SIGNPOSTS
to
LOCAL DEMOCRACY

Local Governance, Communitarianism
and Community Development

Paul Henderson and Harry Salmon

THE LOCAL GOVERNMENT CENTRE

COMMUNITY DEVELOPMENT FOUNDATION
• PUBLICATIONS •

Foreword

This booklet is published jointly by the Community Development Foundation (CDF) and the University of Warwick's Local Government Centre (LGC). The Community Development Foundation is a national expert agency in the field of community development. Its mission is to strengthen communities by ensuring the effective participation of people in determining the conditions which affect their lives. The Local Government Centre is a Research Centre in Warwick Business School, at the University of Warwick. The Centre has a distinctive concern with both the fundamental changes that are taking place in the political, economic and social context of local government, and the implications of these trends for the strategic management of change by local authorities.

Although the views expressed in the following pages are, of course, those of the individual authors themselves, the booklet reflects the coincidence of the interests of both the LGC and CDF in the idea of community governance. This implies, on the one hand, building communities which are empowered and assisted to do things for themselves, and, on the other hand, a 'listening and learning' local government, taking authority from the community to give demo-cratic direction and leadership.

We are, therefore, pleased that Paul Henderson (Director, Practice Develop-ment CDF) and Harry Salmon (Associate Fellow, LGC) have examined different approaches to these themes and brought together key ideas relating to commu-nities and local governance. Their material is challenging and relevant to a wide range of policy-makers, researchers, practitioners and community leaders and we are confident that it will contribute significantly to debate and discussion.

Our hope is that the booklet will be used at conferences, seminars and train-ing courses, and that it will be read and used by commentators on contemporary British society. The intention of both our organisations is to support these processes as actively as possible.

Alison West
Chief Executive
Community Development Foundation

Mike Geddes
Research Manager
Local Government Centre

Community Development Foundation

CDF was set up in 1968 to pioneer new forms of community development.

CDF strengthens communities by ensuring the effective participation of people in determining the conditions which affect their lives through:

- influencing policymakers
- promoting best practice
- providing support for community initiatives.

As a leading authority on community development in the UK and Europe, CDF is a non-departmental public body and is supported by the Voluntary and Community Unit of the Home Office. It receives substantial backing from local and central government, trusts and business.

CDF promotes community development by enabling people to work in partnership with public authorities, government, business and voluntary organisations to regenerate their communities through:

- local action projects
- conferences and seminars
- consultancies and training programmes
- research and evaluation services
- parliamentary and public policy analysis
- information services
- *CDF News*, a six-monthly newsletter
- publications.

Chairman: Eddie O'Hara, MP
Chief Executive: Alison West

If you would like more details about CDF's work, or a copy of our latest publications catalogue, please contact us at:

Community Development Foundation
60 Highbury Grove
London N5 2AG
Tel: 0171 226 5375
Fax: 0171 704 0313
Email: admin@cdf.org.uk
www.cdf.org.uk

Introduction

The election of the Labour Government in May 1997 means that the themes of local governance and community participation will move closer to the centre stage of political discourse and policy-making. How these twin themes are handled in the run-up to the millennium will be critical for the future of local democracy in Britain.

Many people believe that 'community' is a concept which ideologists of both Left and Right raid from time to time in order to bolster their positions. In terms of practical policy outcomes, it is felt, there is little to show for it. Yet in recent years researchers, 'Think Tanks', and commentators have sought to specify the meanings of 'community' and local governance. Coupled with this is a heightened awareness of the dangers of unbridgeable chasms opening up in society.

Our purpose in writing this booklet is to contribute to debates on these matters. We do so for three reasons. First, there is the need for community development to address the new government's agenda: new opportunities, therefore, to re-engage with key concepts and policies which affect people's lives so deeply. We are seeking to articulate some of the principles and experiences of the many individuals and organisations committed to community development. Our intention is to capture the interplay between the weight and wisdom of this 'tradition' and policy concerns of the government: neighbourhoods near to breakdown, alienation of dispossessed people from the political system, uncertainty as to what can be expected from local community action, an awareness of the need to knit together the themes of citizen participation and representative democracy.

The second reason for writing picks up the need to put forward some key questions about the ideas of communitarianism. Does communitarianism understand what is happening to some neighbourhoods in Britain? How, if at all, does it connect with local people's capacity to organise and mobilise? Is it based on questionable assumptions? We know that these questions are being raised by many who are working with and on behalf of local people. They have encouraged us to examine communitarianism because of its separateness from community development thinking.

The third reason springs from a wish to communicate to policy-makers the distinctive contribution of community development to debates on citizenship. In recent years a new vocabulary relating to partnerships and enterprise has emerged. We hear, for example, about the role of the 'social entrepreneur', a hybrid of individualism and corporate responsibility. What is missing from this and other fashionable constructs is the two-fold focus of community development: a clear commitment to supporting grassroots action and encouragement of self-determination and local control coupled with an acknowledgement that strong representative local government can play an enabling role in support of community development. There is an interdependence between the two – we believe the benefits deriving from this dynamic need highlighting.

There are practical implications of recognising the extent to which community development is fundamental to local democracy. While we touch on some of them, our prime objectives are to encourage reflection and fuel debate. We begin by discussing the connections between local democracy and local government, drawing on both the extensive literature and recent initiatives. In Chapter 2 we re-affirm both the centrality of 'community' to local democracy and the need to shake some life into a well-used and often abused concept. We provide a critique of communitarianism in Chapter 3 and present an overview of community development in Chapter 4. In the concluding section we draw the threads of the arguments together.

Hope and optimism are key ingredients of community development and we need to keep hold of them as much in the political and policy contexts as we do when working in neighbourhoods. This booklet has been written with the hope that readers will put effort into extending the analysis of 'community' and local democracy offered here, informed by their knowledge of collective action and activities of residents. Both community and local democracy can make a significant difference to quality of life because good ideas and policies impact eventually, both on professional practice and community life.

1 Local Democracy and Local Government

Now that the effects of Labour's dramatic general election victory have been absorbed, we need to give attention to what some commentators are beginning to refer to as 'a crisis in democracy'. A number of concerns which were being expressed about the state of our democracy have not been resolved by the outcome of the election, and indeed an analysis of the voting figures may deepen some of them.

At the May election just over 71% of us exercised one of our most fundamental rights by electing those who will govern us for another five years. Today almost every adult has that right, though it is denied to homeless people, prisoners and people with serious learning difficulties. The freedom to vote is the essential component of representative democracy that can be traced back to the ancient Greeks.

Democracy is made up from two Greek works – *demos* meaning people and *kratos* meaning rule. In the fifth century the city-state of Athens became famous for the way it was governed. The citizens were regarded as equals, though citizenship did not extend to women and slaves. Citizens enjoyed certain freedoms so long as they discharged their civic responsibilities. They governed themselves but they were expected to participate in the process of law making. There was a balance between rights and duties, and the evidence suggests that the citizens of Athens discharged their obligations with enthusiasm. As we come to the end of the millennium, modern citizens display rather less enthusiasm for the democratic process.

The Reluctant Electorate

Commentators on the 1996 American Presidential campaign referred repeatedly to the apathy of the electorate which they contrasted sharply with the eagerness of people to vote in South Africa's 1994 first non-racial election. Similar comments were made about the 1997 election campaign in the United Kingdom. Often – not very convincingly – the length of the campaign was given as an explanation for the lack of enthusiasm. While in South Africa poor black communities have high hopes that representative democracy can produce a more just society, that hope is no longer shared by many in the US and the UK.

The 1997 general election turnout of 71.3% was the lowest since 1939. This followed three elections in which the turnout had edged up to a high of 77.7% in 1992. In local elections the turnout averages 40% and in May 1996 it was 36%. The proportion of the electorate voting in recent years has not changed dramatically, but we have to go back to the general elections of 1950 and 1951 for turnouts in excess of 80%.

Our particular concerns are the persistently low turnout at local elections combined with the fact that specific groups are under-represented at the ballot box in all elections. Quoting averages hides disparities in voting based upon class, race, gender and age. An analysis of the voting figures for different constituencies and wards shows that the turnout is invariably lower in deprived areas than in those which are affluent. In the recent election, for example, Liverpool Riverside's turnout was 51.9% whereas the two Wirral constituencies had turnouts of 77% and 81% respectively. It is also recognised that large numbers of black people choose not to vote, and it is unlikely that the situation improved at the last election given that black people and the issues which are of particular concern to them were largely excluded from the national campaigns conducted by the three major parties.

A report from the think-tank Demos, written by Wilkinson and Mulgan (1995) on 18–34-year-olds, offers no comfort. MORI carried out a survey for Demos which showed that in the 1992 election only 43% of 18–24-year-olds and 68% of 25–34-year-olds voted, and though this trend was true across all sections of society, it was disproportionally so amongst the most disadvantaged. The Demos report goes on to suggest that young people are 'leading a deepening public detachment from politics'. Given that we have little historical evidence on young people's attitudes towards electoral politics, we cannot rely too much on this particular piece of research, but it does offer a snapshot of current attitudes towards representative democracy. Balancing this, many young people do display an active interest in particular issues.

The alienation of poor and marginalised people from the processes of electoral democracy is particularly serious. In South Africa, as we observed above, poor people are putting their hope in the ballot box. That is how it was here in the 1930s and 1940s, and in America in the 1960s. But today many of the most reluctant voters are to be found amongst what is often derogatorily described as the 'underclass'. They no longer believe that their circumstances will be significantly changed simply by electing a different Party into power. And although Labour's strategy of targeting middle class voters paid off, it did nothing to encourage those excluded from an affluent society to think differently.

Galbraith (1996, p.8) sums up the situation when he observes: 'the rich and the comfortable have influence and money. And they vote. The concerned and the poor have numbers, but many of the poor, alas, do not vote. There is democracy, but in no slight measure it is a democracy of the fortunate.'

Looking for Reasons

There is no single explanation for what is now often referred to as 'the democratic deficit', the failure of many people to exercise their voting rights, and there has been no systematic evaluation of the relative merits of the various explanations that are offered. However, it is likely that a variety of factors – some of which are linked – contribute to people's disenchantment with politics and politicians.

Disenchantment with politicians and political parties

It is common knowledge that politicians have low scores when it comes to ranking professional people in terms of respect and popularity. They have had a bad press, not without reason.

- Sleaze and corruption have figured prominently in recent years, and being told that it is even worse in other countries does nothing to restore confidence. There is a widespread feeling that politicians are 'in it for what they can get out of it' rather than for what they can contribute to the public good.
- Televising the House of Commons has done little for the reputation of Parliamentary democracy. It has allowed the public to witness the charade of Prime Minister's Question Time and the emptiness of the Chamber on most other occasions.
- The failure of Ministers to acknowledge mistakes and to accept responsibility for much of the time that the Tories were in power, and the sophistry and obfuscation in which politicians engage when being interviewed, have all conspired to diminish politicians in the eyes of the public. Widdicombe's belated post-election attack on Howard was an illustration of the failure of Ministers 'to own up' when things have gone wrong.

Centralisation

The electoral process at the local level has been devalued by the way in which the state centres of power and control have been moved further away from the electorate.

In spite of Conservative claims to the contrary, there has been a significant centralisation of power since 1979. Leach et al (1996) say there is hardly a local authority service where the discretionary powers of the local authority were not reduced during the period from 1980–92. This is sharply illustrated by the way in which control is exercised over local government finances. Local authorities can no longer set their own business rate, they have been capped if they set a Council

Tax which exceeded their spending limit, and they are now dependent upon central government for a much higher proportion of their income than in the past. Though progressive councils were, in the past, sometimes forced to trim their spending programmes in deference to reactionary Ratepayers Associations, at least their views were accepted as part of the cut and thrust of local democracy.

If the Labour Government does not restore some of the powers of local government, it is difficult to see how the democratic deficit at the local level can be redressed. Increasingly, citizens are recognising the relative powerlessness of their elected representatives, and this does not bode well for local democracy. Local governance is no substitute for local tax raising powers.

Non-elected bodies

Another dimension to this is the way in which power has been shifted away both from the local authority and the electorate and placed in the hands of appointed bodies. Training and Enterprise Councils, Development Corporations, funding bodies for education and health service trusts are prominent examples of this 1980s and 90s trend. Such agencies now control several billion pounds of public money. The aim is to separate political and managerial functions, but in practice this distinction frequently becomes blurred. It would also appear that such bodies have been at least as culpable of waste and imprudent expenditure as those which are elected. Any democratic accountability through the relevant secretary of state is tenuous, and there is no place for local authority representation on health authorities and health service trusts.

A case could be made for appointed bodies, we believe, when the primary need is for people with certain types of experience and expertise, and when the parameters are clearly defined and the resources controlled are modest. But the creation of what has been described as a 'quangocracy' can do nothing to strengthen people's commitment to representative democracy at the local level.

Alienation

Reference has already been made to the way in which sections of the population are alienated from the political and electoral processes of the democratic system. While Labour's landslide victory at the election was a source of excitement and a topic of conversation amongst large sections of the population, according to some observers, it hardly received a mention on run-down estates, in the tower blocks and in shuttered inner-city areas. In many of these locations, few had voted. No doubt the psephologists will map voting patterns by area, occupational grouping, age, gender and ethnic origin, but it is unlikely that their work will do any more than confirm that electoral politics continue to have little appeal for the most marginalised groups in society. Those who live at the sharp end of inequality have no confidence that any government is going to change radically their situations, and with the exception of the 1945 Labour government, this has been generally true.

At the national level, modern media-driven election strategies are more likely to reinforce this sense of alienation than to reduce it. Sophisticated analytical techniques result in a relatively small section of the electorate being targeted. At issue are marginal constituencies, focus groups and floating voters, but not convincing a million or so disillusioned citizens that it is worth exercising their right to vote.

As we shall argue more fully later, a healthy democracy is dependent upon a strong civil society, a society embracing groups and organisations, in which people enjoy a sense of mutuality. But since 1979 this has been damaged by an ideological approach which has placed an excessive emphasis upon individualistic values. Competition has been stressed rather than co-operation, individual choice has been promoted at the expense of the common good, and politicians have appealed to people's self-interest rather than to their altruism. Now we are paying the price. In *Cities of Pride* (1995), Tyrell refers to the way developments over the last 17 years have led to the increasing 'privatisation' of people's lives, and how this even extends into families. He sees the 'cellular family', where members eat at different times, listen to their own types of music, watch their own TV programmes, and often have their own space, as the ultimate example of this process.

These and other factors will determine how people play out their role as citizens. At the same time, serious attempts are being made to redress the democratic deficit. Ways are being sought to make local democracy more responsive to the people, and these will be outlined below.

Reforming the Democratic System

The search for responses to the crisis in local democracy has resulted in numerous ideas for reforming the system. In summarising these, we will draw upon the final report of the Commission for Local Democracy (CLD) *Taking Charge: The Rebirth of Local Democracy* (1995) and on a research report *Enhancing Local Democracy* (Wahlberg et al, 1995). First, however, we refer to the need for changes in the relationship between central and local government.

Central/local government

We have already noted the constraints imposed on local authorities by central government. If there is to be a 'rebirth of local democracy', then councils must be given greater power, status and independence from Whitehall. One of the ironies is that while the Conservatives were insisting on member states of the European Union retaining control over their own affairs, they were taking away power from local councils at home. The principle of subsidiarity was fought for in Europe, but was not applied in dealings with local government.

If the subsidiarity principle was applied to relations between central and local government, then it would create a favourable climate for rejuvenating local democracy. It could, for example, result in

- local authorities being given back the capacity to raise a greater proportion of their income
- greater control given to local authorities over how they allocate their resources, with fewer grants being tied to specific projects
- allowing councils greater freedom to experiment and innovate if they were granted 'powers of general competence' in line with the *European Charter on Local Government.*

These are suggestions which are widely supported by those who speak for local authorities and by those bodies which want to see a strengthening of local democracy.

Constitutional changes

The CLD's report puts forward recommendations which would involve changes to the way in which local councils are elected. A system of Proportional Representation (PR) is considered essential to a healthy local democracy. European experience suggests that it increases the incentive to vote. The Commission also wants to see the election of a Leader or Mayor once every three years. In addition, they recommend annual elections, the creation of smaller wards and more councillors, thus reducing the ratio of electors to those elected.

Finally, we list mechanisms and procedural changes which could influence the level of citizen involvement in the process of governance and also increase the possibility of people voting.

Citizen participation

The CLD recommends that local authorities produce an annual Democracy Plan which would set out decentralisation initiatives and proposals to involve citizens in the process of governance. Below we list some of the measures which they believe could encourage a greater level of involvement:

- referenda and ballots
- citizens' juries
- mediation groups to encourage dialogue where there are conflicts of interest
- referenda on particular issues or proposals

- groups of citizens to monitor services
- user involvement in service provision
- community development
- officer support for community groups in deprived areas
- use of 'phone-ins'.

There are also suggestions for making it easier for people to vote. These are:

- setting up very local polling stations
- extend voting over two days – possibly a weekend
- improving the registration level from its average of 95%.

Wahlberg et al (1995) list seven types of 'new democratic structures' (NDS) ranging from neighbourhood forums to focus groups or task teams. The writers explore the implications of NDS in respect of their composition, representative legitimacy, relationships with councillors and their powers. They also introduce a wider European perspective using examples from France, Denmark and Germany. There will be references to examples of NDSs below.

Local Governance and Local People

The cumulative effect of changes imposed upon local government since 1980 has compelled councils to look afresh at their role, and to examine how they can most effectively discharge the functions which remain under their control. One of the positive things to emerge from a period of turbulence is that councils have had to establish a closer and more open relationship with those they represent.

During the early 1990s the phrase *local governance* was introduced into our vocabulary. It is used increasingly to describe the changing nature of the relationship between local authorities and their citizens. Instead of controlling from the centre, many councils are beginning to define their role in terms of facilitating and orchestrating developments in their area. Increasingly they see their task as bringing diverse interests together to enable new projects get off the ground.

Local governance consists of a complex web of agencies and organisations drawn from the public, private and voluntary sectors plus the groups which reflect the needs and aspirations of local people. Major employers of labour and large voluntary organisations have usually been able to exercise some influence on decision making through lobbying and informal contacts, but the process has been far from transparent. The emphasis now is upon creating more open links between important contributors to the economic and social fabric of an area, and extending these links to take in the plethora of other bodies and groups that also impact upon the well-being of an area. It is a response to the realities of a more pluralist distribution of power, resources and influence in society.

Benington (1996), in strongly supporting the move towards local governance, offers a theoretical representation of how it contrasts with more conventional ideas about the relationship between politics, administration and the electorate. In his alternative model, there is a close interaction between civil society, the political arena and public administration.

Our primary concerns are with collective ways for people to share in local governance and with how citizens can most effectively become involved in participatory democracy. The danger for groups based upon interest or locality is that they become absorbed into local governance in such a way that they have little influence or freedom. This risk will be referred to in later chapters, but now we want to look at ways in which local authorities are seeking to engage with local citizens.

Local Government Initiatives

In *Enabling or Disabling Local Government*, Leach et al. (1996) provide a useful categorisation of the kind of strategic choices local authorities are making. Each choice has particular implications for the way in which councils relate to their citizens. They identify four:

- direct service provision
- commercial approach
- community governance
- neighbourhood approach.

The first two place the emphasis upon customer and consumer relationships. In the second two, the stress is upon citizenship and democracy.

Clearly the choice which is made will be influenced by the council's ideological stance. In practice, of course, the choices and their consequences are not usually as well defined as this categorisation suggests. With the first two choices, there is likely to be more transparency than in the past, but the focus remains upon representative rather than participatory democracy. People are seen as electors, and as customers. Where councils opt for either community governance or the neighbourhood approach, there are opportunities for developing a creative – though not always comfortable – relationship between citizens and those elected to govern. It is these choices which are compatible with community development.

In these local authorities, some measure of decentralisation is becoming the norm. Geddes (1996) provides helpful examples of what is happening in different parts of the country. Broadly, decentralisation takes two forms: the decentralisation of services and the decentralisation of decision making. These are clearly not incompatible with each other and can, in fact, be combined. In practice, the first can be a step towards the devolution of varying degrees of control to a local level.

There is a third form of decentralisation, but this has come about as a consequence of legislation passed by the previous administration with the aim of further reducing the powers of local authorities. This has sometimes involved the transfer of assets, as with Housing Action Trusts (HATs), or of management, as with the Local Management of Schools (LMS).

Decentralisation of services

Having begun in the 1970s, decentralisation of services is now well established. Housing and Social Services have usually been the first to be located nearer to users. It is now common for local authorities to emulate Walsall's initiative where, in the early 1980s, 33 neighbourhood offices were opened. Birmingham, for example, has a comprehensive system of neighbourhood offices, but this has meant that it has been harder for locally controlled advice and welfare rights centres to obtain funding, and few survive. Undoubtedly, the financial constraints on local government means that cost becomes an important and sometimes a crucial consideration.

Service decentralisation obviously involves organisational and administrative changes within local authorities, and affects internal decision making. Indeed, in some authorities the emphasis has been on developing internal structures to make departments more responsive to local needs, rather than on the physical decentralisation of services.

Responses to decentralisation have been mixed. Easier access to services has been welcomed, but problems are not always resolved any more speedily. In some instances, lack of resources has meant that requests for services are rejected with more grace than in the days of Town Hall bureaucracy. Many of the most marginalised citizens preferred independently run advice centres to council run neighbourhood offices and 'one stop' shops. The strong advocacy role which workers in locally controlled centres can exercise is missed as is the scope for representing the collective needs of particular groups.

Devolution of decision making

The two best known examples of decentralisation linked to devolution and decision making are Islington and Tower Hamlets, and these are compared and contrasted in *The Politics of Decentralisation: Revitalising Local Democracy* (Burns et al, 1994). There are now a number of others including Bradford, Harlow, North Tyneside, Kingston and Somerset. Some councils have been forced to draw back from radical ventures into the devolution of decision making as a result of financial or political pressures.

Tower Hamlets was a radical experiment based upon the Liberal Democrats' commitment to devolution. Area committees of local councillors were set up and given extensive powers over policy and resources within their areas. Mechanisms were created enabling local people to be involved in the process of governance. Unfortunately, in the 1990s the area has been bedevilled by racial politics, and the situation reached crisis point when a British National Party candidate was elected to the Isle of Dogs ward in a local by-election in 1993. Though the councillor was rejected in May 1994, it exposed one of the dangers of devolution of control to a ward level. In the 1994 election, Labour took control and since then this form of devolution has been abandoned.

The Islington experiment in decentralisation began in the early 1980s and has attracted much attention. It has been less radical than the Tower Hamlets scheme, but it has stood the test of time better. Power and services have been decentralised to local offices, but in contrast to Tower Hamlets, a strong central core has been retained. People at the local level are represented on high-profile neighbourhood committees, but the committees are mainly consultative and have no control over policy or mainline spending.

Many other local authorities seek to engage people in decision making at a neighbourhood level. They use methods ranging from public meetings through to community forums and citizens hearings. Some have strategies for continuously involving people through partnerships; others make sporadic attempts to organise consultative committees or take soundings from local leaders.

Currently, it is impossible to assess the effectiveness of these initiatives in improving attendance at the ballot box. On balance, it seems unlikely that on their own they will make much difference. Though a number of community workers have moved into politics, there appear to be few examples of local people standing as councillors as a result of their involvement in community politics.

Starting with the People

So far we have dealt with proposals for rejuvenating our democratic system which require action by government at both the national and local levels. We have also seen how local authorities are increasingly decentralising their services, and are seeking to involve citizens in the process of decision making. The focus has been on 'top-down' initiatives. From a community development perspective there are serious flaws in this approach and there are also limitations to its effectiveness. In the final part of this chapter, we will turn to ways of addressing the democratic deficit through local initiatives. We will begin by looking at two different interpretations of citizenship.

Citizenship

In *Community and Public Policy*, Butcher and Mullard (1993) refer to citizenship as a 'contested concept'. They go on to quote Ungerson (1992) who says that the one thing which is clear about it is that 'it is always concerned with the relationship between individual and the state'. Prior et al (1995, p.100), who deal with the notion of citizenship in depth, distinguish between citizenship based upon consumption, and citizenship 'as membership in a political collectivity or community embodying different, and potential conflicting values'. The contest between these two interpretations of citizenship is crucial to the debate about democracy.

The Conservative Government encouraged an individualised consumerist notion of citizenship. It did this mainly by subjecting public services to the discipline of the market, and by emphasising the 'rights' of consumers by introducing charters. Consumers become customers who are supposed to have choice. Those local authorities which have opted for direct service provision or for the commercial approach have taken the same route.

York City's Labour controlled Council launched its charter in 1988, and the government followed. In 1991 John Major introduced the statement on which the Citizens Charter was based and by 1994 there were 23 government-sponsored charters in operation in the UK. They are concerned with individual rather than collective rights, and they privatise citizenship by ignoring the possibility of collective responses to deficiencies in the provision of services or goods.

There are positive features to the consumerist approach to citizenship. It is good that service delivery is being improved, that consumers have rights and are being consulted about their requirements, but these are not the measures which will revitalise local democracy.

When in 1989, Douglas Hurd, as Home Secretary, sought to widen the notion of citizenship beyond charters and consumers and relate it to society – the 'society' which Margaret Thatcher said did not exist – he referred to 'active citizenship'. The images behind the term, however, are of individuals who give to charity, do good to others, sit on the occasional committee and serve on a non-elected body. This intervention by Hurd did little to broaden the concept of citizenship.

We turn now to the stronger version of citizenship which is about participation in the processes of democracy. It draws on what Prior et al (1995, p.19) describe as the 'civic republican tradition', and is sustained through reciprocal relationships between citizens.

Civil society

The notion of 'society' that recognises we are partly the product of a set of complex relationships, is now widely accepted. In other words, we are more than a collection of individuals. The related concept which has come back into circulation recently is that of 'civil society'. This is most simply understood as a web of autonomous associations – groups and organisations – which sometimes have the potential to influence public policy. They stand outside the state though they function within the country's political system.

It is significant that the growing concern about the state of representative democracy in the UK has come at a time when the bonds of civil society are weak. The figures published for many of the organisations which have traditionally contributed to the enrichment and well-being of society show a steady decline in membership, and this has often been sharpest in blighted urban areas. These are the same areas that have low turn-outs at elections.

An extensive study carried out in Italy seems to indicate that communities with high levels of involvement in local groups and activities can help to generate the conditions for a lively and effective democracy.

Putnam (1993) and his colleagues have researched the effectiveness of regional government in Italy over a 20-year period since its general introduction in 1970. They have discovered remarkable differences between the northern and southern regions. In the North the regional administrations have been more efficient and the areas become more prosperous than the South, and people relate to their regional governments in the two parts of the country in very different ways. In the North people use their regional councillors much less than in the South and when they do, it is usually about policy and issues. In the South councillors are approached mainly on personal matters with people seeking favours and preferential treatment.

The vast differences between the performance of regional governments led Putnam to examine carefully the differing social contexts and how these had been shaped over a long time. They found that in the North there was a strong republican tradition, whereas in the South there was a tradition of patronage based upon authoritarian relationships. In the North there were strong bonds of mutuality sustained through dense networks of civic involvement. There was a wealth of 'social capital' which did not exist in the South. Putnam and his team were persuaded by the evidence that the explanation for the contrasting levels of effectiveness achieved in the northern and southern regions of Italy were primarily attributable to these differences.

Though the historical legacy is very different, comparisons can be made with some parts of Britain, and the study is particularly relevant to the Labour Party's proposal for regional development agencies and possibly assemblies. It also reinforces our view that people's shared political experiences, and the nature of their communal relationships, are as likely to determine whether or not they vote as will any reforms to the democratic system.

Campaigns and struggles in a very different political and cultural context to that of Britain can remind us of the need to remain alert to finding ways of creating a vigorous civil society at grassroots level. For example, over the last few years several community development organisations in Britain have worked with new, democratically controlled organisations in Hungary. Many of these make strong connections between the participation of local people and the creation of a strong civil society. For those people in Britain involved in supporting Hungarian organisations and groups, this has been an inspiring experience. It has reaffirmed key principles of community development, and been a reminder of the close links between civil society and democracy.

The need to work at strengthening the bonds of civil society is of paramount importance. A rich, vibrant, pluralist society provides the conditions in which democracy can flourish. All the worthy ideas put forward for solving our democratic malaise will fail unless they are accompanied by a resurgence of values of mutuality and shared responsibility. Local authorities will be frustrated in their attempts to involve local citizens in civic affairs, unless they can draw on positive experiences of collective endeavour.

Both communitarianism and community development are seen by their advocates as being ways of injecting new life into civil society. The rest of our analysis will be devoted to examining these claims, and to assessing what contribution – if any – these two very different approaches might make to reducing the democratic deficit and to generating a sense of mutual responsibility. But first it is necessary to examine the concept which is central to both these approaches – 'community'.

2 The Importance of Community

The idea of community has absorbed the energies of researchers and writers to the point where they have risked the exasperation and boredom of readers. But the result has been the accumulation of a large body of knowledge about communities and networks. It is based on the work of a range of individuals, from anthropologists and sociologists to community workers and local leaders.

More recently, we have witnessed a surge of interest in 'community' among national politicians, think tanks and local government leaders. 'Community' is an idea that will not go away. People wrestle with it because of its profound significance. This can be seen in the way that increased recognition has been given in recent years to defining community in terms of peoples' shared interests and identities as well as in terms of locality. Community as identity has been particularly significant in discussions of race and gender. Helen Meekosha provides an important analysis of these discussions: 'Practitioners and activists are increasingly finding themselves concerned with the implementation of equality of opportunity, anti-discrimination, and access and equity. Respect for difference and acknowledgement of identity are also part and parcel of contemporary strategies' (Meekosha, 1993, p. 172).

We have no intention of adding to the literature on community, or of summarising the overarching themes. However, it is important to emphasise the key ground rule for any discussion of community: the need to separate out its different conceptual meanings. The way in which enthusiasts of community have used the term loosely has, with some justification, laid them open to criticism from academic writers, not only on the grounds of vagueness but also because it leads to policy mistakes. Benington (1974, p. 260) drew attention originally to the way in which community was used as a kind of aerosol 'to be sprayed on to deteriorating institutions to deodorise and humanise them'. The habit has grown worse. Frazer (1996) is critical of the way the term is applied, and questions the emphasis placed upon it by local government. Other writers point to the ways in which communities can exclude others, and how they can be oppressive for people within them. Pahl (1996) wants to replace the notion of community with that of the 'friendly society', and points to Coleman's (1957) highly critical assessment of the term. Cohen (1997) grounds his critique of community in our contemporary

16

situation, and in the way in which the term is used in relation to Blair's vision of a 'New' Britain.

Burns et al suggests the following distinctions:

- *Community as heritage* – the expression of a common cultural tradition or identity
- *Community as social relationships* – the patterns of interrelationship reflected in kinship, neighbouring, mutuality, support and social interaction, often deriving from the residential base
- *Community as the basis of collective consumption* – an appropriate aggregation of the needs or demands of groups or neighbourhoods for local public goods (libraries, transport, environment etc.)
- *Community as the basis for the most effective production and provision of local public goods* – whether these be provided by private, public or voluntary sectors (including the community itself)
- *Community as the source of influence and power from which is derived empowerment and representation – or their converse* (Burns et al, 1994, p. 225).

It is the last of these which relates most directly to community development and local governance. It derives from political science and takes seriously the idea of empowered communities.

Focusing on the connections between community and empowerment arises from our conviction that politicians and policy-makers need to better understand not only what is happening to communities but also what is being done by them. The action of local people is a missing dimension in debates about rights and responsibilities. Local action gets to the heart of this booklet's message: community is a dynamic concept, and it matters intensely to many people. Local involvement and citizenship is forged out of their commitment. That is why this chapter focuses on the meaning of 'community' within a community development framework. First, however, we set community in the wider context of social exclusion.

Social Exclusion

Nearly one household in six in Britain is living below the poverty line. Employment growth in old industrial regions such as South Yorkshire and the West Midlands is among the most sluggish in Europe. We do not need to provide a litany of woe to make the point that, primarily because of poverty and unemployment, certain groups in British society live on its margins.

Not all poor people live in deprived neighbourhoods, and the focus of policy-makers on local area approaches has been criticised. Rural poverty, in particular, tends to be dispersed and hidden. The social implications of poverty can be denied by rural people themselves. A research report on disadvantage in rural Scotland comments that the most challenging finding is that rural people's subjective assessment of their poverty or disadvantage tends to be at odds with objective definitions such as income level and transport costs (Shucksmith et al., 1994). Overall, however, the evidence is that the gap between poor neighbourhoods and others has widened. The former are areas which are 'increasingly stereotyped as housing of last resort and as a source of crime and welfare dependency'. They suffer from both "post code discrimination" and a moral backlash against what is described by some commentators as an "underclass" divorced from the values of the rest of society' (Taylor, 1997, p. 64). This clearly raises issues for local democracy.

The concept of social exclusion has only recently gained currency in this country only relatively recently. It is a broader concept than poverty because it goes beyond income and material resources to include inability to participate effectively in society because of personal powerlessness. It was first developed in France in the early 1970s and later became important in the anti-poverty programmes of the European Union. The concept is important because it:

- highlights the idea of distance within society between the 'haves' and the 'have-nots'
- points to the existence of economic, political and social forces outside the control of the individual. It suggests a process taking place as a result of decisions and non-decisions of many institutions
- relates to groups of people – people from ethnic minorities, women, elderly people, people with disabilities – who, on a definition of poverty based only on income, might otherwise not be considered to be outside the main currents of society:

'Exclusion suggests that someone or something is doing the excluding. It makes a definite connection between rich and poor, the included and the excluded. It is not a passive state. It is not self-generated' (Russell, 1995, p. 96).

Any discussion of community has to be grounded on an awareness of the links between the situations facing people in deprived neighbourhoods and the action or inaction of the rest of society. The connections between excluded communities and 'comfortable' Britain need to be examined; so too does the impact of decisions made by national and international policies of governments and corporations on local communities. 'Community' means nothing if it remains a remote, arid concept or if it connotes only nostalgic warmth. Worse still, however, would be to understand it as being politically neutral, which raises the need to connect it with an analysis of why some people are excluded from participating in society.

At the same time it is crucial to avoid aligning the concept of exclusion with notions of helplessness. This is a point emphasised by Max Farrar in his study of Chapeltown in Leeds. In addition to showing how the black community in this inner city area has been excluded from developments in the rest of the city, he draws attention to the role played by community organisations: 'The long history of independent political action by Chapeltown's black organisations indicates the high resolve of black people to maintain the momentum for inclusion' (Farrar, 1996, p. 311). There are human resources that can be mobilised to benefit the community in the most disadvantaged neighbourhoods.

Social inclusion is, perhaps, a more appropriate term for community development than social exclusion because of its suggestion of involvement – we return to this point in Chapter 4. Here it is important to note the inseparability of community from the issue of participation and the commitment of both community development and anti-poverty programmes to supporting the participation of excluded people, recognising their strengths and capacities: 'Inclusion gives a message of people joining in activities, debates and decision-making, not of being shut out' (Henderson, 1997, p. 6).

Understanding communities is also inseparable from questions of social justice: 'Self-respect and equal citizenship demand more than the meeting of basic needs: they demand opportunities and life chances' (Commission on Social Justice, 1994, p. 18). Tensions and fear will often become evident in some neighbourhoods through crime, violence and vandalism. Conflicts can be exacerbated by class and racial differences. Some of the causes of these social problems lie in economic and social policies that have had the effect of increasing inequalities. This is a form of injustice not because people have had their legal rights taken from them but because people have been disempowered. A form of apartheid has taken a hold on British society in relation to community: the majority who live in relatively pleasant areas have become separated from the minority of neighbourhoods where very different conditions apply.

The signs are that this trend will be very difficult to reverse, partly because of the exhaustion of people who have little power and partly because of the way in which the majority in society is pulling away from the minority. It tends to be excessive self-interest on the part of the majority that drives the two apart. For many people, the election of the Labour Government in May 1997 provides a real opportunity to reverse this dominant value. Recognising and strengthening community will need to be central to the process.

Chaos or Cohesion?

The riots which took place in 1991 in several cities were, according to Campbell (1993), as much *against* the community as they were *about* it, young unemployed men destroying estates rather than communities seeking help. This theory is linked to the assumption that there was an inevitability that neighbourhoods would fall into crisis because of the new economic order begun in 1979. We believe that the causes of the conditions existing in many urban and rural areas of Britain go back further than that. We also think that the problems facing local people are more complex than is implied by a perspective which concentrates on so-called ghetto estates.

Politicians and policy-makers must be encouraged to rediscover their commitment to 'community' not through grasping at last-ditch measures to stave off riots but as a result of having a better understanding of what is happening to neighbourhoods. What do we mean by this? How can politicians and policy-makers make use of what is known about community from both the considerable research which is available and from the experiences of people who live in fragmented communities?

We suggest three angles. First there has to be *analysis*, close study of existing data about communities. This needs to be done at both macro and micro levels: the wider national and international context and the extent to which the global economy affects communities (employment, environment, population movement); the local context and evidence from case studies and research pointing to some essential components of stable communities (jobs, safety, involvement for example).

Second is *listening* to the experiences and voices of communities – specific spatial neighbourhoods (an estate, a cluster of streets, a village) as well as interest and identity groups (people with disabilities, young people, Black groups, women's networks etc.). This is an obvious way into understanding community but despite the availability of well-tried methods and techniques, it is often done very poorly: public meetings not planned properly, for example, or promises about feedback or follow-on action not kept. And yet the views of people about community are an important source of information. It is only by listening to them that differences within communities will be brought out – the range and variety of items – but also some issues, such as safety and environment, that are important to all groups.

Finally there is *involvement*. The theory of partnership tells us that communities should be involved in regeneration schemes on an equal basis alongside the statutory, voluntary and private sectors. The reality is different. Too often community groups receive information about plans for their area too late. Their involvement is partial and only rarely do professional agencies make significant efforts to draw in a range of community interests. It tends to be the same faces round the table. Policy-makers need to ensure that community involvement is accepted as integral to good practice by agencies committed to partnership working. We are not there yet.

If the ways in which communities function are not taken more seriously, we are likely to see more instances of crisis situations arising. Sometimes this will take the form of riots, attacks on the police and other outbreaks of violence. More often it will be exhibited by attitudes of apathy and resignation among local people in the face of social problems – unemployment, poverty, drugs misuse, crime, vandalism – over which they feel they have no control and which they are sceptical of the capacity of agencies to tackle.

It is misleading to take community for granted. It is this misguided notion which, as we will show in the following chapter, makes the claims of 'communitarianism' questionable. 'Community' has to be struggled for. We need to be able to specify its significant features. That is why the idea of social cohesion – recognition of the need to hold society together – is directly relevant to any discussion of local democracy and participation. It is aligned closely with the concept of social inclusion and is central to thinking within the European Union. It shifts community away from being a remote abstraction to being a live, dynamic concept which must be at the heart of policies for local democracy. This is, we realise, a tall order, but if the importance of community is not continually put under scrutiny, calls for citizen involvement and community-based economic and social programmes will become increasingly disingenuous. They will be built on shifting sands and, in the end, fail to connect with what really matters: the lives of people who, in a myriad of ways, together constitute 'community' – feelings of togetherness or solidarity, being willing to act together on a continuum ranging from small informal networks to large-scale community organisations.

'The 1990s have seen the rise of a "communitarian" movement, which sees in local communities the means to redress the problems both of the market and the state. They see in the community the means both to provide the welfare that the state can (or will) no longer afford and to reverse the moral decline which many see in modern-day society. But while the renewed emphasis on community is welcome, we must beware of seeing community as a magic wand, especially in those areas which have been marginalised by economic development. If it is to be reversed, society will need to invest in change and not leave it to those who have been pushed to the margins' (Taylor, 1997 p. 69).

3 Communitarianism

Since early 1995 there has been a remarkable surge of interest in communitarianism, an import from America. It started when Demos, an independent think-tank, provided a platform for Amitai Etzioni, the American sociologist, whose seminal book, *The Spirit of Community* (1993) was published here with a British preface in 1995. Through conferences, publications and numerous articles in periodicals and the broadsheet press, communitarianism has become a lively topic of conversation, and has attracted the attention of a range of people.

Communitarianism's main appeal is that it has offered a middle way between the rampant individualism of recent years, and the kind of socialist statism which is now out of favour. Its emphasis on the family, and its vision of communities accepting a greater measure of responsibility for their own well-being, have an obvious appeal to those who complain about the lack of parental discipline and the dependency culture. Politicians who have themselves been extolling the importance of the community and stressing the role of the nuclear family, find that it chimes with their own beliefs. There are those in local government who turn to communitarianism for ideas and inspiration as they seek to engage local people in the kind of neighbourhood initiatives referred to in Chapter 1.

In this Chapter we provide an introduction to communitarianism, and explore its limitations as a basis on which to establish greater social cohesion.

What is Communitarianism?

We are posing a question to which there is neither a short nor definitive answer. Communitarianism consists of a collection of ideas, perspectives, values, exhortations and moral platitudes. Etzioni's own brief answer to the same question is: 'We are a social movement aiming at shoring up the moral, social and political environment. Part change of heart, part renewal of social bonds, part reform of public life' (1995, p.247). But he follows this with a 'preamble' which takes up 14 pages (pp. 253–267)! In *The New Golden Rule* (1997) he develops his ideas on communitarianism in relation to both community and morality, and deals with some of the criticisms which have been levelled at it.

Inevitably, if we tried to summarise in a paragraph or two something that is both as amorphous and as complex as communitarianism, we would do its advocates a disservice. The term is already being used with the same casualness as the word 'community', and it often does little more than give a community-oriented gloss to what is being said. Instead, we will trace its theoretical roots, identify key themes and offer a brief critique. Other writers on the subject will be mentioned for those readers who may wish to explore it further. Examples of communitarian practice will be given, although, interestingly, few are available.

Communitarian theories

In the *Spirit of Community* (1993), Etzioni makes little reference to the origins of communitarianism. However, in the preface to the British edition (1995), where he maintains that communitarianism is not an 'American import', he says its roots sprout from ancient Greece and the Old and New Testaments. In an article in the *New Statesman* (Etzioni, 1995b), he includes a paragraph on the origins of communitarian ideas, and in his latest book he draws on the thinking of a distinguished group of philosophers who explored communitarian ideas in the 1980s but often without unequivocally committing themselves to communitarianism. The theoretical debate has been kept alive in the 1990s by people like Gray (1995, 1996), Frazer and Lacey (1993) and Taylor (1995).

From this ongoing debate we can pick out a number of ideas which form the theoretical basis of communitarianism. They all have practical implications.

- The individual, the self, is seen as being embedded in communal relationships, and is the product of her or his social environment. We cannot be separated from the society which has shaped us.
- Individuals can only flourish within the context of rich forms of common life. Even our health can improve when we are caught up in shared enterprises, and have some control over our own situations.
- The emphasis on intersubjective relationships shifts the focus away from both the individual and the state. It avoids the excesses of individualism without slipping into a form of totalitarianism.
- As in ancient Greece, citizenship carries with it civic responsibilities. Modern versions of republicanism emphasise the will of the people, and self-rule based upon bonds of family, friendship, shared history and the common good.

Communitarian values

Values such as reciprocity, solidarity, good neighbourliness and mutuality are important to communitarians, and arise naturally out of the core theoretical themes. They are, of course, shared by many other people, and today few would take exception to them. But communitarians have a lot more to say on values, and it is this which gives rise to the criticism that they are moralistic in their approach. Values are key themes in Etzioni's writings, and they figure prominently in Tam (1996).

For Etzioni, 'the golden rule' is about preserving a balance between social order based on moral values, and the autonomy of individuals and small groups. Without the first, we slip into anarchy; but without autonomy, we create 'authoritarian villages' or worse. Maintaining equilibrium between what might appear to be opposites is seen as being an essential ingredient of a 'good society'. Stressing equilibrium is partly Etzioni's response to the common criticism that communitarians emphasise responsibilities rather than rights.

Three general points can be made about communitarians and values:

- Stress is placed on the need for communities to legitimise values, and to exert pressure to ensure that they are upheld.
- Schools are seen as having a large measure of responsibility for moral education.
- Little is said about the values which should be practised by corporate bodies, public agencies and people holding high positions in society.

The communitarian agenda

Etzioni's communitarian manifesto was adopted by 70 leading Americans drawn from both conservative and liberal traditions in November 1991. It contains three main themes which have struck a chord with a similar range of people on this side of the Atlantic. They have to do with responsibility, the family and the community.

Responsibility is central to his philosophy. He maintains that in every society a balance must be established between rights and duties, and he claims that in America the pendulum has swung too far towards the assertion of rights. He believes that the social fragmentation which is a feature of American life today is largely due to the failure of people to exercise social and moral responsibility. In his view, the situation has been made worse both by the welfare-liberalism of the 1960s and 70s, and the free-market conservatism of the 1980s. While one ideological approach allowed people to be ruled by their own moral inclinations and to reject traditional constraints, the other encouraged competition and greed. Both militated against the development of a sense of responsibility.

Communitarianism is concerned with inculcating in ordinary people a sense of responsibility for their own well-being, the family and the communities to which they belong.

The *family* is where responsibility to others begins to be expressed. Etzioni is paramount among the advocates of the virtues of the nuclear family. 'Communitarians', he says, 'call for a *peer marriage* of two parents committed to one another and their children, with both parents equal in their rights and responsibilities' (Etzioni, 1995b, p. 24). While accepting that some single parents look after their children well, he goes on to comment: 'I'd rather give a child three parents than one'.

He identifies with those who would make divorce harder, and would discourage single women from having children. The title of Etzioni's book, *The Parenting Deficit* (1995a), reflects his belief that – at the very least – this is an important contributory factor in social problems such as drug abuse, criminality, school truancy and anti-social behaviour. Though he emphasises the importance of the contribution of both men and women in parenting, the reader is left with the impression that Etzioni still sees it as primarily the woman's task to be available to meet the child's needs. Communitarians place the primary responsibility for moral education firmly in the hands of parents. They see stable families where children have been taught to accept responsibility for their own actions as the foundation stones for strong and active communities.

There is a progression in communitarian thinking from personal responsibility through to a *community* of communities. Etzioni is fond of talking about a communitarian nexus, which seems to mean a diversity of communities neatly nesting into each other. At the edges of communitarianism, there is a utopian vision of a world community.

Given the extent to which politicians, people involved in local government and voluntary agencies are talking about the importance of community, it is not surprising that Etzioni and his followers have struck a rich vein in their emphasis upon building and strengthening communities. To politicians anxious to reduce public spending, it is good news to hear about a movement which believes that communities should look after their own welfare and only resort to public bodies for help as a last resort. It must seem a happy contrast to the early 1970s when community action was increasing demands upon public resources.

Communitarian practice

Community development has been practised in this country since the late 1960s. It has a body of trained practitioners, and there are numerous case studies and research reports evaluating its effectiveness available both in the US and the UK. Communitarianism is different. It is a product of the 1990s. It is not about skills and – so far as we know – does not seek to have 'communitarian practitioners'. At the moment, there are few examples of what it looks like in practice. However, more UK-based material is likely to become available over the next year or two.

In 1995 the UK Communitarian Forum which had recently been established published its first annual newsletter entitled *Democratic Communities*. Its editor is Henry Tam, the Deputy Chief Executive of St Edmundsbury Borough Council, who is one of the most vigorous exponents of communitarianism in this country. Both Tam (1996) and Atkinson (1994) have written books which refer to communitarian practice. The early issues of *Democratic Communities* contain a bewildering range of bits and pieces, many of them contributed by academics or people glad of publicity for their organisations. Many of the items seem unrelated to communitarianism except that they have a link – sometimes tenuous – with 'community'.

Etzioni (1995a) provides examples of what he regards as communitarian action. He points out that half of America's Emergency Medical Technicians are unpaid volunteers, and he sites a programme whereby more than 400,000 Seattle area residents had been certified to perform cardiopulmonary resuscitation by 1988. In a different kind of illustration he describes how a local initiative in rubbish clearing in the South Bronx was stopped by the heavy handed intervention of the police.

Communitarians show a particular interest in crime prevention. Etzioni refers to crime watch schemes, and the use of groups who engage in anti-crime patrols. The Guardian Angels of New York have had their counterparts operating in London. It is also interesting that the most fully recorded piece of communitarian activity in this country are the citizens' patrols in Balsall Heath, Birmingham. They began as a local initiative to stamp out prostitution and drug dealing in an inner-city area. At first, police had reservations about the scheme, but are now working in co-operation with local leaders who claim that drug dealers and prostitutes have been driven off the streets. Probably it is also significant that an early book from the communitarian stable is entitled *Punishment, Excuses and Moral Development* (Tam, 1996).

Phillips (1995) cites Easterhouse and Balsall Heath as good examples of communitarian practice. Atkinson (1994), who is a communitarian enthusiast and worked in Balsall Heath during the late 1960s and 1970s, provides additional information about locally-based developments which can be described as communitarian in character. As in Etzioni's work, the school is given prominence as a key institution.

The difficulty with the examples quoted is that there is nothing very distinctive about them. Some of the examples of locally-based activity in this country had their origins in community development of the 1960s and 70s. They are now being rebaptized into the communitarian movement! Etzioni's examples are replicated here in organisations such as the St John's Ambulance Brigade and schemes like Neighbourhood Watch. Probably more significant than the activities which are now termed as being communitarian in character are the kind of things which are missing.

The Communitarian Deficit

People with very different ideological perspectives have embraced communitarian ideas. A conservative version of communitarianism is presented both by Harris (1992) and Willetts (1993), whereas Dennis and Halsey (1988) have put a socialist gloss on it. Given their current views on the family, and the fulminations of Dennis (1996) on young men, sex and crime, it is easy to see why Etzioni's themes would appeal to them.

Of course, advocates of communitarianism will claim that this is one of its virtues. It cuts across ideological allegiances. Mulgan (1995) describes it as an escape from ideology to ethics. The original group of academics reacted to what they saw as the polarisation of the ideological debate, and Etzioni was eager to stress the endorsement of his communitarian manifesto by people from both the right and the left of the political spectrum.

We would argue, however, that this is a reflection of its weakness. In seeking to escape from ideology, communitarianism resorts to a consensual mode that avoids dealing with basic conflicts of interest. The results are that it lacks an adequate analytical framework, it masquerades as a solution to problems it does not properly understand, and diverts attention away from causes to symptoms.

Though communitarianism purports to offer a middle-way between the private and public approaches to problems, Etzioni's version can easily be hijacked by right wing extremists at both the national and local levels. At the national level, a House of Representatives led by a Newt Gingrich can translate the 'parenting deficit' into punitive legislation against one-parent families, and at the local level, self-policing activities can degenerate into physical and verbal abuse of prostitutes. In the UK, the communitarian reaction to single parents can lead to approval for decisions by the previous government and supported by the present government to cut the £5.65 lone parent premium payment to income support claimants from April 1998, and not pay non-means tested benefit to new lone parents from the same date.

The communitarian agenda based upon personal responsibility, the family and community is a popular one. It appeals to politicians and policy-makers. But the way in which communitarianism deals with these matters is inadequate. Of course people should behave as responsible citizens, but they also have rights. Etzioni (1995b) says that rights and responsibilities are two sides of the same coin. In practice, he separates them. He makes a judgement about whether a society needs a dose of rights or responsibilities. '[I]n China', he says, 'I stressed the need for individual rights. In the United States, I stress the need to shore up the sense of individual and social responsibility.' In that case, should not the same principle apply when dealing with individuals, families and communities? If fairness is to operate, then account must be taken of people's social and economic circumstances.

Even if we accept the need for a greater emphasis on duties and responsibilities, the communitarian case is flawed by its failure to address the social responsibilities of governments, public agencies and private corporations. Charles Derber (1995), one of Etzioni's main American critics, points out Etzioni's failure to both stress the social responsibilities of multinational companies, and draw attention to their large scale abuse of property rights. As a key principle of communitarianism, social responsibility should be applied not only to people, families and communities, but also to all those bodies which affect the lives of ordinary people.

Etzioni's stress on the nuclear family has proved to be particularly popular with political leaders and some observers of the social scene, but it is the point on which he is most vulnerable. Difficulties arise because he fails to take account of the vastly changed social and economic contexts within which families now function. Demaine (1996) accuses Etzioni of substituting vague pleas for 'what ought to be' for 'decades of academic research into education and sociology' (p. 12), as well as showing no awareness of critical assessments of communitarianism in relation to the issue of gender.

Frazer and Lacey (1993) began in 1988 by seeing some resonances – ideas of reciprocity, solidarity and fraternity, for example – between feminism and communitarianism. It prompted them to examine the links from a philosophic point of view, and this led them to the conclusion that 'Gender remains of conceptual irrelevance for communitarian political theory: it is either ignored, or gestured at in a way which assumes that gender issues can be incorporated without conceptual modification' (p. 158). Etzioni's 'gesture' consists of one reference to feminism and none to gender in *The Spirit of Community*, where the family is discussed at length and two brief references to feminism in *The New Golden Rule*.

The fallacies and prejudices revealed in Etzioni's defence of the nuclear family and his treatment of what he describes as the 'parenting deficit', are sharply exposed by Campbell (1995) and Murray (1996). Campbell argues that his critique of parenting is directed primarily against mothers. She points out that women frequently have to compensate for absentee fathers, and even in two parent families, often have to supplement the household income in addition to caring for the family.

According to Murray, Etzioni is wrong to attribute the parenting deficit to the absence of parents because of work. Unemployment and male criminality have been found to be more important in determining the quality of parenting. Drawing on research by the Centre for Micro-Social Change, she points out that full-time working women in the 1980s spent more time with their children than full-time home-makers in the 1960s. Dennis and Erdos (1992), surprisingly, have also fallen into the trap of imagining that way back in the 1950s fathers spent much more time with their children than they do to-day. Etzioni pays no attention to the politics of time debate which shows – amongst other things – that women in employment still spend far more time with their children and doing housework than fathers working similar hours.

Though communitarianism strongly stresses the importance of the family and the responsibilities of parents, there is a striking absence of any references to the policy changes – some of them comparatively small – that are required in order to provide better conditions for bringing up children. Both Campbell and Murray identify the changes which are needed. But this is symptomatic of more fundamental weaknesses in Etzioni's form of communitarianism.

Hughes (1996) deals at some length with the interest which conservative communitarians – amongst whom he includes Etzioni and Dennis – show in crime, and how it has been singled out for particular attention. Reference has already been made to communitarian practice's association with vigilante-type activities both in America and in the UK. The border line between acceptable forms of crime prevention by local people and more proactive measures against those engaging in anti-social behaviour is not easily maintained, and some communitarian responses to crime are at least questionable. Etzioni (1995, pp. 140–41), for example, advocates the naming and shaming of people guilty of offences, and such ideas are beginning to find a sympathetic hearing on this side of the Atlantic (Leadbeater, 1996). It can also be argued that communitarianism is 'tough' on the perpetrators of crime, but weak on the 'causes of crime'.

Structural change does not figure in communitarianism. A 'bottom-up' approach is commendable, but it loses credibility and also contact with reality if it does not take account of the external constraints on human development. The economic dimension, for example, is ignored. Gray (1996) draws attention to the failure of communitarians to say anything significant about the way in which globalisation and economic policies generally have contributed to the decay of communities. Community development, on the other hand, has always recognised the need for socio-economic changes which cannot be brought about simply through a 'community based' approach. In writing from her perspective as a community worker, Wilson (1995) makes the same point in response to an article by Tam (1995) on communitarianism.

In *The New Golden Rule* (1997), Etzioni returns to the argument about rights and responsibilities. He again deplores the explosion of rights in the Western world, and argues that the constant quest for greater liberty does not necessarily contribute to a 'good society'. He stresses again to the importance of accepting our social responsibilities, but still does not widen this to include the responsibilities of governments, corporate bodies and powerful elites. The focus continues to be solely on ordinary citizens. In *The New Golden Rule* he does accept that the gap between the rich and the poor is too wide, but to go on and suggest that 'dialogue' is the way to achieve a less unequal society is facile in the extreme.

This failure to face up to the questions of power and inequality means that communitarianism's message to marginalised and excluded groups appears hollow and cynical. It comes across like this to Margaret Simey (1995). She is highly critical of the communitarian approach, and observes that it sounds like a 'conversion project' for the 'preservation' of an existing way of life. She adds:

'We long to be responsible but are consistently thwarted by our relegation to the status of a dependent underclass.'

Given the importance that is attached to the notion of community in Etzioni's programme, we might expect that the term would be applied with some rigour. That it isn't is all the more surprising seeing that Etzioni is an academic sociologist. Instead, communitarians use 'community' uncritically, and without addressing the questions which are being raised in the debate about locality, neighbourhood and community, and without referring to the glaring contrasts between different communities in terms of power, resources and opportunities. Apart from referring to different types of community based upon place, work or interest, its meaning is not subjected to any kind of serious analysis. In this publication we have tried to establish a better balance between analysis and application – analysis in the previous chapter and application in what follows.

4 Community Development – The Way Ahead?

Unlike communitarianism, the community development movement in Britain has not, with one or two exceptions, promoted its principles and methods. Mostly it has adopted an informing and responsive stance: enthusiastic to involve enquirers but averse to evangelism and the hard sell.

One explanation for this modesty has to do with resources. It has become increasingly hard to keep funds flowing to support grassroots community development work. National bodies too, part of whose brief is to explain community development to other people, have had to exist on minimal resources.

Another explanation can be found within the community development process itself. Community workers are concerned that through this process, local people should be empowered, and this should speak for itself rather than be mediated through others. The result, however, has been that, in the public domain, community development has tended to sell itself short. There has, we suggest, been progress at getting community development understood and recognised within policy-making organisations. That is not the same, however, as having achieved a popular profile.

- Community development is about local people doing things for themselves with the proviso, discussed in Chapter 2, that communities are not expected to do everything.
- It is a process of empowerment and change undertaken on a collective basis. Community development is also an intervention – by community workers and others – designed to help people organise and to respond to problems and needs that they share.
- It is misleading to look for the results of community development only in communities. Evaluation of community development needs to take into account the way communities relate to the world outside and the way the world outside relates to communities (Barr et al., 1996, p. 9).

These statements begin to demonstrate the extent to which community development is integral to the building of strong communities. It is also an essential part of creating a participatory democracy. That is why, when discussing the importance of 'community' in Chapter 2, we suggested that the concept of social inclusion rather than social exclusion fits best with community development. Not only does it convey the idea of people joining in, it also highlights the commitment of community development to working predominantly with oppressed and marginalised people. While community development can be practised in any kind of community, the focus is usually on involving those who have been excluded from participating in society. By looking in turn at the practice, strategies and policies of community development we shall demonstrate the important contribution that community development can make – alongside a range of policies and programmes – to the building of viable, meaningful and inclusive communities.

We shall also draw attention to some of the conceptual and practice weaknesses of community development. In the final chapter we shall argue that community development:

- takes account of social and economic structural factors in society
- engages with the issue of power and the relative powerlessness of marginalised groups
- recognises the importance of the issues of class, race and gender
- is alert to the existence of conflicts within neighbourhoods
- has a record of progressive democratic action.

The extent, however, to which the track record of community development supports these claims must – we would readily agree – be scrutinised closely.

Practice

Three themes stand out from an overview of community development practice in the UK over the last 30 years. First is the commitment to grassroots activity and action. Despite its acute awareness of the structural causes of deprivation and powerlessness, community development has been characterised by a neighbourhood focus. Yet it can be argued that it has been the emphasis on operating at the neighbourhood level which has limited community development. There are very few problems which can be resolved only by local people. 'Communities cannot turn around estates on their own. Regeneration requires investment from government and other partners' (Taylor, 1997, p. 65). By maintaining its emphasis on very local, face-to-face work, community development in the past underplayed the vital contributions of agencies' policies and resources. Both neighbourhood work *and* organisational change are needed in community development.

Community groups tend to be wary of the policy emphasis on partnerships because the latter mostly originate as 'top down' initiatives and are therefore able to control how groups participate. Informing this alertness to the threat of incorporation lies community development's experience of thousands of neighbourhood projects. Projects in which participants share the same locality and where the contact with a community worker is very direct: face-to-face, day-by-day on the streets, in a community hall or neighbourhood centre. Social planning as a form of community development, with its implied distancing from local people, has always been suspect.

The second key feature of practice is it's breadth:

- support of centre-based activities
- helping to provide local services
- negotiating with the local authority and other agencies about provision of services
- campaigning for improvement of neighbourhoods
- supporting local economic development schemes.

Community development is generic in that it can adjust its methods and skills to meet the requirements of this range of activities and action. In order to respond to this range, specialist organisations exist for particular sectors. The organisation Community Matters, for example, supports community centres and community associations, the Tenants Participation Advisory Service tenants groups etc.

The third theme is the multi-issue capacity of community development practice. The following list gives a sense of this feature:

Issue	*Examples of practice*
Housing	Tenants associations
Employment	Community businesses
Environment	City farms
Poverty	Credit unions
Architecture	Community facilities
Transport	Community transport schemes
Health	Women's health forums
Community care	Disabled people groups
Children	Safe play areas
Crime prevention	Community associations
Drugs prevention	Parents' groups

Some of these issues, notably housing and employment, have been mainstream to community development practice for a long time. Others, such as drug prevention and community care, have emerged more recently. Different professions have become aware of the need to open up the community development dimension which creates a challenging dynamic. It results in a process of re-energising community development. A similar process can be observed in the way that community development is applied in different kinds of neighbourhoods. One aspect of this is the urban-rural continuum: having been associated for a long time almost entirely with urban neighbourhoods, community development is now also practised widely in rural areas and small towns. The other aspect, noted earlier, is the way in which community development has become relevant to networks and communities of identity and interest which are not wholly neighbourhood-based.

Equally important as the range of issues covered by community development is its capacity to work across them: it has a linking and integrating function which is invaluable to practice. The phrase – somewhat dated now – used to describe this is the 'holistic approach'. It is based on knowledge of how local people experience social problems. People tend not to keep problems in discrete compartments which mirror central and local government departments but rather to make connections between them. Community development speaks to this experience. It seeks to link, for example, anti-poverty measures with regeneration and health issues. It is both a cross-cutting and unifying approach. Its effectiveness here, however, is dependent on the presence of key factors locally and at the level of policy.

Local Factors

The key local factor in community development is trust.

- Trust building among members of community groups is essential for any effective community development practice. This is grounded in notions of solidarity, collective or group responsibility. People join a community group voluntarily and undertake, implicitly or explicitly, to be accountable to group decisions.
- Often the skills of a community worker are needed to facilitate this process of forming and building an organisation. Trust is also needed between this person and local people and, especially in areas where local people feel they have been let down by external agencies, this can be very hard to achieve.
- On both counts – within a group and the group-worker relationship – the crucial condition for creating trust is time. Community development is not a 'quick fix' activity or intervention and never could be. It has been the failure of policy-makers to take this point seriously that has led to frustrations and unrealised expectations.

It is not that advocates of community development are asking for an entirely open ticket: they are as capable as anyone of setting objectives, putting down markers. The point is that if the process of working with local people is to be done properly, then community workers and others need to be given the time and space in which to operate. Otherwise they will be prevented from maximising one of the most exciting aspects of community development: the education and development of individuals resulting from their experiences of community development – learning through doing. Tony Gibson refers to it as the discovery of bargaining power: 'first their time and common sense; then gradually, their growing knowledge of the way things *could* be' (Gibson, 1996, p. 281).

Policy Factors

The evidence of the last 30 years is that, if community development is going to be effective, a number of additional factors must be in play. Most of these require policy decisions by agencies, a point brought out in a recent major international study of community development. The research found that, for participation to be an effective community development value, it is necessary for most of the following factors to be present:

* an open and democratic environment
* a decentralised policy with greater emphasis on local initiatives
* reform in public administration
* democratisation of professional experts and officials
* formation of self-managing organisations of poor and excluded people
* training for community activism and leadership
* involvement of non-governmental organisations
* creation of collective decision-making structures at various levels that 'extend from the micro to the meso and macro levels and link participatory activities with policy frameworks' (Campfens, 1997, p. 461).

Each one of these factors is of major significance; taken together they show how community development cannot be expected to work in a vacuum. At different stages in the community development process they have to be on the agenda. In the final part of this chapter we shall argue that community development has addressed policy questions only recently. Its full potential for achieving change has not been realised because of its late arrival at the policy table.

Strategies

There is a creative tension within community development between the principle of remaining open to the ideas and priorities of local people, and effectiveness. We have emphasised above the point that needs defined by local people is of central importance in community development – the building and ownership of an agenda by local people. The downside of this is that community development is liable to be pushed and pulled in too many directions; it can become all things to all people, having minimal impact.

To handle this tension it is essential for community development to be highly strategic: devising clear aims and objectives, against which outcomes can be measured, while retaining its commitment to local accountability. Acceptance of the need for strategy has given community development the confidence to discuss with agencies the real benefits it can bring to local communities: it can present itself on what it can deliver as well as on its inherent values. The strengthening of community development in this way explains why it has gained widespread recognition as a form of planned change.

There is an awareness that community development will be ineffective unless it relates to, or feeds into, more political and economic movements. It was this stance which was at the heart of the structural analysis developed by the Community Development Projects in the early 1970s, reflecting a concern with the longer-term goals of transformation: 'If community participation and empowerment are to contribute to such longer-term goals, then strategies do need to be formulated within the framework of alternative critical economic, social and political perspectives' (Mayo and Craig, 1995, p. 10). In general, however, community development in the UK has not followed through the agenda for bringing about structural socio-economic change. Rather, it has chosen to operate at the more pragmatic level of influencing the strategies of a range of agencies, particularly local authorities.

The Association of Metropolitan Authorities published reports (AMA, 1989, 1993) which underlined the extent to which local authorities could maximise use of the strategic opportunities of community development. This commitment to supporting community development is being continued by the new Local Government Association. A strategic approach was taken by a few local authorities such as Strathclyde Regional Council in the 1970s (see Barr, 1996b) and a number have followed a similar course since then. Sheffield, Swindon, Cleveland/Redcar and Salford are examples of authorities which, despite having had to cope with severe cuts, have retained their commitment to community development.

Increasing numbers of local authorities, too, have committed themselves to strengthening community networks and infrastructures as well as helping individuals and groups. This relates to the changing relationship between local authorities and residents discussed in Chapter 1. An important influence on the development of support for networks has been research which provides evidence for the existence of a community sector: 'The community sector is larger, longer-lasting and more influential in the life of the locality than is realised by public and policy-makers alike' (Chanan, 1994, p. 3). The formation of the Community Sector Coalition in 1993 signalled to local authorities and voluntary organisations the need for them to give this recognition to small community groups.

There is some evidence that this message is being heeded, although most authorities still tend to be reactive rather than strategic in their approach.

There has, however, been some movement at central government level which has had the effect of emphasising the strategic role of community development. The most obvious manifestation of this has been the community participation aspects of the Single Regeneration Budget Challenge Fund. Partnerships making bids to both the urban and rural Challenge Funds are obliged to show how the strengthening of communities will be built into their plans. This has provided an unprecedented opportunity for community development (CDF, 1997). Above all, it has obliged community development to function effectively at a strategic level with local authorities, partnership bodies and government regional offices.

Regeneration has certainly been one area in which community development has flexed its muscles. In the local authority context, it complements the interest and experiments in service decentralisation. Admittedly it is funding-led – the motivation of partnership bodies to engage with community development has been funding requirements rather than a sudden conversion to citizen participation. In this sense, community groups are rightly wary both of the intentions and capacities of partnerships. Some of their attempts to involve community groups have been seriously flawed.

It is important to emphasise that strategy in community development is not confined to working within the framework of government funding regimes and local authority-dominated partnerships. Pluralism, and a willingness to try out new strategies, have both been important characteristics of community development. Here we note four contrasting strategies.

Planning for Real was the brainchild of Tony Gibson of the Neighbourhood Initiatives Foundation. It is based on people's need to make use of their spatial perception. Gibson piloted a series of packs using 3D layout: people could see the potential for change in their neighbourhood by moving parts of the cardboard model around and, as a result, placing demands on officials. 'The traditional consultation process was turned on its head. Instead of the professionals coming in to consult you, the residents, and then going away to decide unilaterally what might be best for them, it was the residents who were consulting the experts to tease out the range of options that might be open in dealing with any issue' (Gibson, 1996, p. 129). Planning for Real caught on and, over the last 20 years, has been used widely in the UK and other countries. The Neighbourhood Initiatives Foundation has used this strategy with many communities, notably on the riot-torn Meadowell estate in Newcastle. But it is more than a technique. It forms part of a framework that leads to participation and dialogue – a strategic response, at grassroots level, to economic and social problems.

Community Organising is based on the ideas and experiences of Saul Alinsky and the work of national organisations in the USA, notably the Industrial Areas Foundation. It is currently being established in the UK, with churches taking the organisational focus. It is a way of mobilising large numbers of people around issues. It makes use of confrontational tactics, usually across an entire city or town. Emphasis is put on careful planning and rehearsal before action, and on evaluation.

Advocates of Community Organising believe that their approach represents one of the few responses to social injustice and poverty in the UK in the 1990s. They are critical of community development, believing that, in its search for funding and partnerships with established organisations, it has lost its radical 'edge' (see Henderson and Salmon, 1995). Community Organising is, therefore, a strategy for grassroots participation which contrasts significantly with other strategies.

Anti-poverty strategies increasingly include a strong community development dimension. This reflects an awareness of the excluding effects of poverty. Being poor means being deprived of enough money to live properly. As we noted in Chapter 2, it also means being prevented from participating in society, and anti-poverty work has turned to community development as a strategy for inclusion. The anti-poverty projects supported by the European Commission, especially those in the 1990–94 programme, were a significant influence. The attention given to the social rights of citizens – and how excluded people are denied these rights – and the extent to which social exclusion permeates virtually every aspect of peoples' lives, are two ideas explored during the programme which have special relevance to community development.

Community development plays an important part in increasing numbers of local authority anti-poverty strategies. It also underpins the approach of several voluntary organisations, notably Oxfam which is developing a UK poverty programme drawing on participation techniques used in developing countries. It will be important over the next few years to monitor the effects of this mobilising role of community development. Curtin (1996) in a discussion of communities and rural poverty in Ireland, suggests that it cannot be assumed that community development activities necessarily address poverty issues. He argues that evidence is inconclusive as to whether community efforts to alleviate rural poverty should be focused on the most disadvantaged or whether the gains to poor people are ultimately greater when emphasis is placed on involving the 'whole' community and increasing the resource base and opportunities for all.

Local Agenda 21 strategies are being implemented by local authorities, following the 1992 Earth Summit in Rio. They constitute an important part of the environmental action agenda, and the extent to which they are underpinned by the themes of participation and community action is very noticeable.

Roome (1993, pp. 205–206) has identified three reasons why there is a congruence between community development and green perspectives:

* the educative function of community development
* community development as 'a lever for personal and collective awareness'
* community development's organisational capacity.

We are witnessing a process of mutual learning and integration between community development and environmental organisations. In 1996, for example, Community Matters and several environmental organisations produced a pack aimed at encouraging environmental action by community groups (Creighton, 1996). The concept of sustainable development – lasting benefits to local communities and effective citizen participation – is putting pressure on economic regeneration agencies to rethink many of their assumptions. This is of obvious importance for children and young people. The variety and extent of initiatives by them signify messages of hope (Hart, 1997).

The last two of the four strategies outlined above illustrate how community development can become part of a range of issues that are of central importance to the future of British society. And it can play a linking role between issues, notably between anti-poverty strategies, environmental action and participation.

The increased effectiveness of community development practice has come about because adopting a strategic approach has been seen to be crucial. It means that community workers and other practitioners can be clear and realistic about what they are doing, and communicate this to managers and policymakers. They are also able to share their aims and objectives with the community groups which they are supporting. There should be no mystique about community development. On the contrary, it is important that the practice and theories remain highly accessible.

The need for community development to work strategically is demonstrated by plans being made to provide training opportunities for managers who have no background in community development (Thornton, 1996). It is also reflected in the commitment of time and energy given by community development training organisations, notably the Federation of Community Work Training Groups, to strengthening training opportunities for members of community groups and unqualified community workers. A number of organisations are currently proposing the formation of a National Training Organisation. Its capacity to work at all levels will be critical.

Policies

We have argued that, unlike communitarianism, community development has devised more sophisticated strategies and analyses of how communities function and strategies for working with them because of its awareness of the complexity of change. The litmus test will be what it does with this recognition. Will it simply use it to obtain resources? Will it become incorporated by the agendas and priorities of powerful agencies? Can it retain its questioning, challenging spirit? Can it keep hold of the sense of being accountable to local communities? These questions apply principally to community development's work on government policies and to the voluntary sector. They also relate, more indirectly, to work with the private sector and to the policies of trusts and foundations.

Government

Community development organisations have always been hopeful that the Home Office unit responsible for supporting the voluntary and community sectors would play a co-ordinating – even advocacy – role across government departments, on behalf of community development. The evidence for this happening, however, is slight, probably because of the smallness of the unit within the overall context of Whitehall. Even when it was moved, in the last year of the Conservative administration, to the much smaller Department of National Heritage (now Department for Culture, Media and Sport), its interest in community development seemed to relate almost entirely to intra-departmental concerns rather than inter-departmental ones. (Within days of coming to power, the Labour Government moved it back to the Home Office.)

Community development is on the agendas of other departments, albeit sometimes under a different label. We have seen already how, under the auspices of the Department of the Environment, Transport and the Regions (DETR) funding bids by partnership agencies are obliged to include community involvement. The idea of local 'capacity building' has attracted considerable interest among civil servants responsible for regeneration programmes (Skinner, 1997). On a smaller scale, the DETR has also recognised community development through support for environmental initiatives.

Interestingly, the most explicit commitment to community development within government is to be found in the Northern Ireland Office. Lead responsibility has been assigned to a Voluntary Activity Unit and an interdepartmental group has been established. The origins of this commitment are to be found in a the Community Development Review Group which, in the early 1990s, undertook a widespread consultation process. An appreciation of both the role and support needs of community groups, plus an opportunity for dialogue between the various stake-holders, have been important ingredients.

The relatively small size of Northern Ireland may have helped. The same may be true for Scotland where community development and community education have gained widespread recognition among local authorities and within the Scottish Office (see Barr et al., 1996c). The latter, as well as supporting community education, also pump primed the Scottish Community Development Centre, a partnership between CDF and Glasgow University. Given the vulnerability of community development when public expenditure cutbacks occur, this kind of commitment is significant.

Elsewhere, notably among the large Whitehall departments other than the DETR, policy commitments to community development are more difficult to achieve. The Department of Health has supported research and dissemination on the scope of a community development approach to community care (Barr et al., 1997), the Department for Education and Employment is working on the proposed National Training Organisation, the Home Office Central Drugs Prevention Unit has arranged community development consultancy for drug prevention teams, the Department for International Development arranged a seminar on community development in the UK for all its social development advisers. Yet these and other examples of community development working at a policy level with government departments are isolated initiatives. They do not relate to an overall policy framework.

Voluntary sector

Community development is widely recognised by voluntary organisations and churches. A large number of Councils of Voluntary Service and Rural Community Councils have an ongoing commitment to supporting community development in their areas. Some of them target resources for innovatory community development initiatives – Durham and Northumberland Rural Community Councils, for example, have both set up large community work teams in former coalfield communities, using European funding.

Examples of a policy commitment to community development can be found in some of the specialised voluntary organisations, notably those focusing on work with and on behalf of children. Barnardos, The Children's Society and Save the Children all recognise the relevance of community development to their work and, in varying degrees, build it into their programmes. While most Social Services Departments, and even some Social Work Departments in Scotland, have abandoned both community development and community social work, the child care organisations have sought to hold on to it because they can see the importance of helping children to be part of neighbourhoods. Bob Holman, writing about neighbourhood work on Glasgow's Easterhouse estate, points to the vulnerability of families living in poverty and makes the case for community development: 'Neighbourhood groups are frequently located near such families and their services can contribute to alleviating hardship, loneliness and exclusion' (Holman, 1997, p. 105). Play organisations and initiatives concerned with children's safety in communities also see the need for a community approach. The 1989 UN Convention on the Rights of the Child has been an important stimulant for this area of work (Henderson, 1995).

Church-based community workers have been important advocates for community development, both within the churches and outside them. The reports *Faith in the City* (Archbishop's Commission on Urban Priority Areas, 1985) and *Faith in the Countryside* (Archbishops' Commission on Rural Areas, 1990) were important milestones, drawing attention to the considerable experience of church-based community development and arguing for its expansion. The Church Urban Fund has enabled a large number of Anglican churches to appoint community workers, and there have been similar commitments by the other denominations, such as the United Reform Church.

Private sector

The private sector came on to the agenda of community development organisations approximately 10 years ago. Its interest has been centred mainly on economic development. In addition, companies' commitment to supporting community projects has tended to be in areas where they have factories or large offices. The economic focus reflects companies' concern to see poor communities become more viable. Many of them recognise the need to invest in communities in order to bring about regeneration – 'Prosperous back streets make for prosperous high streets' as one company put it.

There is a congruence here between the private sector and government policy, with companies playing an active part in many partnership schemes. This helps to explain the focus of companies on areas with which they have a connection. While several of the large multinational companies have developed a national perspective, the vast majority have not. Accordingly, there is little evidence of companies and community development organisations working together at the policy level. Economic development is another matter, with the organisation Business in the Community playing a linking role between companies and communities.

Traditionally, companies have often been on the receiving end of community development, in the sense that their practices – air and noise pollution, environmental hazards, discrimination – have been challenged by community groups. The way in which this 'mind set' has changed is a remarkable turnaround, and there is no reason why the dialogue between community development organisations and companies should not develop further, moving from funding and partnership matters to policy questions. Companies such as Northern Foods, IBM, Laing and the Co-operative Bank are already opening up this area.

Trusts and foundations

For over 20 years, the Gulbenkian Foundation played an active policy role in the community development field (see Thomas, 1996). Have other trusts and foundations taken its place, interested in helping to support and shape community development?

No one trust has filled the vacuum. The Joseph Rowntree Foundation has probably come closest to doing so, having shown an increasing commitment to the theme of resident participation in estate regeneration programmes (Stewart and Taylor, 1995), but it has not engaged with the community development occupation in the way that Gulbenkian did. Possibly it and other trusts would argue that the government's Voluntary and Community Unit now has a more explicit role in this area.

On the other hand, the policy contribution of trusts continues to be important in relation to particular developments. For example, CDF obtained core funding from several trusts to help establish offices in the North of England and Scotland, the Joseph Rowntree Charitable Trust has played a key role in supporting community development in Northern Ireland, and the establishment of Community Organising in the UK has depended heavily on active support and involvement of trusts. Trusts have also seen the need to support community development on an issue basis – poverty, for example, and rural issues – and the growth of regionally-based trusts, such as the Tyne and Wear Foundation for the North East, has also been significant.

Community development's engagement at policy level with government, voluntary organisations, the private sector and trusts has changed over time, usually in response to a changed 'climate' – positive or negative – in any one of them. We have argued that, within community development as a whole, there is a greater acceptance of the need to work within the policy framework of government – central and local – than previously. In this significant shift there are elements of survival and opportunism. Yet underlying it is a worked-out perspective on how change is achieved, a realisation that if the conditions of Britain's most deprived and powerless communities are really going to change, then any serious strategy has to operate at policy levels as well as at the grassroots.

In a sense, therefore, community development has grasped hold of the policy agenda. It still has to demonstrate, on the basis of evidence, that it can deliver. What is important, however, is that, despite facing very testing political and funding conditions, it has succeeded in building a reasonably solid practice and organisational base. Community development's 'strength in depth' is illustrated by:

- the improved coordination of regional and national community development organisations through the Standing Conference for Community Development
- the development of evaluation methods which means that community development's impact can be measured in terms of effectiveness and efficiency
- a capacity to think and act creatively and put forward new ways of responding to contemporary issues.

The two key issues on which community development has performed less successfully have been those of race and gender. To the external critic, the way in which white and Black community development organisations and networks exist alongside each other but, with a few exceptions, do not work together must be very evident. It is as if there is a stand-off between the two, nervous of entering into dialogue for fear of the emotion likely to be generated. At a general level, it can be argued that this mirrors the relationships between white and Black communities. A more telling and accurate critique, however, is that Black groups feel themselves to be excluded by mainstream white organisations.

On the question of gender, despite universal recognition that, in most instances, it is women who provide the energy, commitment and leadership in community groups, there has been a reluctance to pursue the strategic and policy implications. This is highlighted in a report prepared by Oxfam for the Joseph Rowntree Foundation on gender and urban regeneration:

> 'Almost all the mainstream literature (outside socialist feminist or equalities writing) is silent on the issue of gender, despite the fact that everyone agrees that it is women who are mostly involved in community regeneration' (May, 1997, p. 40).

In the final chapter we discuss the need for community development to address these and other challenges if its potential for playing a lead role in the development of local participatory democracy is to be realised.

5 Conclusions

The themes explored in this booklet are complex and interrelated. They are relevant because of the social and political context in which we are living. There is a deep sense of unease about the lack of social cohesion, and commentators talk increasingly about the breakdown of traditional bonding mechanisms and about the decline of long-established institutions. For the life-time of four Parliaments we have been subjected to an ideologically driven political programme in which free market capitalism has reigned supreme with few checks and balances. This has resulted in widening inequality, a shrinking welfare state and a decreasing role for local government, with the accompanying growth of non-democratic and therefore unaccountable bodies.

The persistent stress on the 'individual' has meant that the cement which holds people together in society has been seriously eroded. The constant emphasis on competition, personal choice and individual freedom has resulted in a loss of collective values. Society has become fragmented, and there is little sense of belonging to 'one nation'. A sizeable section of the population is now alienated from wider society, and some have been so infected by the culture of acquisitiveness that they resort to anti-social ways of acquiring what others enjoy in abundance legitimately.

During the 1990s, however, there has been a change of mood. The majority of people are disenchanted with the operation of unbridled market forces, and have started to recognise that the preservation of public goods such as education, health and welfare is essential to the maintenance of a strong and cohesive society. They have had enough of market utopianism and are looking for an alternative vision.

Participatory Citizenship

It is encouraging that people now recognise the importance of services available to all without conditions being imposed at the point of access. Though people do not use the words, it suggests that they are interpreting citizenship in terms of common interests and reciprocal responsibilities. When voters say they would be willing to pay more tax in order to have better public services, they probably now mean it, and politicians in the two main political parties have underestimated the extent to which the mood has changed. If this is the case, then the climate is right for promoting the stronger version of citizenship referred to earlier – based upon involvement in a vigorous civil society – and which is more fully developed by Prior et al (1995). Indeed, unless this is the case, then the hopes of politicians and officials for an increased role for communities, and for the participation of people in the processes of governance, are not likely to be realised.

The concept of citizenship has traditionally had a low profile in the UK. There is the historical legacy of regarding people as 'subjects of the sovereign', and then only granting the full rights of citizenship to the population in stages. Marshall (1950) describes the way in which citizenship has developed over time, and he identifies three types of citizenship rights which were the product of different periods of history. They are legal rights, political rights and social and economic rights. These rights are not immutable and in the absence of a Bill of Rights can be withdrawn or amended.

Political parties have concentrated on trying to persuade citizens to participate in electoral processes, and it is only recently that a wider definition of participation in the affairs of governance has become popular. In Chapter 1, we showed how this is increasingly being taken on board by local councils as they adapt to their new circumstances.

In practice, there is a close link between social and economic rights and people's participation in political processes. Those who are denied their social and economic rights are less likely to engage in both representative and direct forms of democracy. Geddes (1995) traces the links between poverty, exclusion and local democracy, and argues that particular attention must be paid to devising ways in which the most marginalised groups can be drawn into democratic processes.

An inclusive and active form of citizenship requires a favourable political climate and a lively civil society. The hope is that the change of government will have contributed one element to this equation. For the other, we return to the constellation of ideas around the popular notion of community.

Community, Communitarianism and Community Development

These terms have been dealt with at some length in earlier chapters. Now their relevance to the present debate about democracy, citizenship and governance must be assessed.

Community

Earlier we sought to set the term within a context, and we have endeavoured to use the word in a reasonably disciplined way throughout the publication. We have avoided an inflated view of its importance, and would urge politicians and others not to place a burden upon it which it cannot bear. However, we continue to believe that communities based upon place, common interest or identity can contribute to giving our fragmented society greater cohesion, and can enrich the lives of those who belong to them. They are essential components of civil society. It is part of the function of governance to harness these diverse communities in the pursuit of the common good.

Communitarianism and community development

In this concluding chapter we want to assess the respective merits of communitarianism and community development as ways of rejuvenating civil society. However, in order to provide a sense of balance, it is worth noting that they draw on similar theoretical roots and have common characteristics.

- They both reject liberal individualism or individualistic theories of human nature.
- Communitarianism draws on theorists who maintain that the individual is socially constructed: in other words, s/he is the product of social, cultural, institutional and communal factors. Community development also recognises the importance of these factors, but would usually also include economic considerations and emphasise the significance of class.
- They share a common belief in the potential for bringing about change through people working together within their own localities or spheres of interest.
- Both communitarians and community development practitioners operate on the basis of values of mutuality, interdependence and shared responsibility, and have a commitment to developing local leadership and decision making.

Though communitarianism and community development sound some of the same notes, there are also fundamental differences between the two approaches. Below we summarise ways in which they differ.

- Community development sets its work within a wider socio-economic context: communitarianism pays little attention to the way in which communities – like people – are also shaped by external forces.
- Community development faces up to the question of power and recognises the relative powerlessness of marginalised groups: communitarianism is strangely silent on the subject, and has little experience of working with excluded minorities.
- Community development sees the need for structural and institutional changes which are beyond the scope of local action: communitarianism is silent about the need for wider changes and tends to uphold the *status quo.*
- Community development appreciates the importance of the issues of class, race and gender though – in practice – it has sometimes been tentative in its

work around race and gender. Communitarianism shows little interest in these themes, and is particularly vulnerable on the rights of women.

- Community development takes account of conflicts within neighbourhoods and between different factions within groups: communitarianism has an idealised view of communities.

- Community development has a long record of being radically progressive and democratic: communitarianism's inclination is to be conservative and authoritarian.

There are, of course, other important differences.

Community development is concerned with *rights* as well as responsibilities. Indeed, community development often works with groups – for example, people with disabilities or homeless people – around rights issues. Etzioni would be more concerned about rights in China than he would in this country where he thinks there is already an adequate provision of rights. And unlike communitarianism, community development does not adopt a moralistic stance on the state of the nation's family life.

Crime is a serious problem, but so are unemployment and homelessness, and yet as we noted in Chapter 3 it is crime which claims the attention of communitarians. It is this issue which has given communitarianism a reputation for moral authoritarianism. Though community development practitioners frequently have more direct experience of living and working in areas affected by high levels of crime than communitarians, they have a more rounded and balanced approach to the problem. While appreciating the seriousness of the issue, they also try to look at the problem in a wider social, environmental and economic context. In their work with local groups, they seek to tease out a range of constructive responses, but they do not advocate simplistic or negative ways of dealing with a complex problem.

The previous chapter showed that there is now a reservoir of community development experience on which policy-makers can draw, and showed the range of agencies engaged in the practice and promotion of community development. It would be a serious error of judgement if policy-makers were to ignore the lessons of community development in favour of experimenting with the version of communitarianism which has been peddled in this country. Neighbourhoods should not be used as laboratories for testing communitarian ideas.

Community development is a tried and tested way of working with people, and is in a position to contribute important insights into the debate about participatory democracy and the ways in which civil society can be strengthened. It has much to offer on the community aspects of local governance, but it also has to face challenges of its own. Taylor (1995) identifies three:

- how to release people's energies without exploiting them
- how to respect 'difference' whilst organising around common interests
- how to make local action relevant beyond the neighbourhood (pp. 108–109).

We would add three more:

- how to recover the capacity to communicate experiences of communities and community development to others
- how stronger links can be made between white-dominated community development and Black organisations
- how community development organisations can place the issues of social exclusion and alienation from the traditional political system higher up their agendas.

Local governance and community development

If the efforts of local authorities to develop new forms of governance involving voluntary organisations and communities based upon interest, identity or geography are to be successful, then – we emphasise again – a necessary prerequisite is a vigorous civil society. Hughes (1996, p. 28) talks about a 're-awakening of a concept of a civil society as a space to be populated by an active citizenry'. In those areas of the UK where there has been a long history of communal groupings, the necessary conditions already exist, but there are now few such areas. There are other localities where groups and networks seem to develop spontaneously and with no assistance from outside. But there are many urban areas beset by decay and poverty, where there are few signs of an active civil society, or little interest in representative democracy. In those situations, there needs to be a sustained application of the principles of community development.

Reference was made in Chapter 1 to the kinds of initiatives that have been taken by local government to make itself more accessible to local people, and to engage them in consultation or even in some measure of decision making. Attention has also been drawn to the inadequacy of policies based on individual rights and choice. 'Exit options' are about the citizen as a customer or consumer, and are based upon the idea that the individual can *choose* to walk out of one door and through another providing a better service. Usually, this bears no relation to reality. Options based upon 'voice' are more conducive to the creation of a dynamic civil society in that they provide opportunities for collective action about inadequate services. It means that local authorities must be prepared for conflict as well as co-operation.

Governance, in many ways, demands more from local authorities than central government. It requires a change of style and approach throughout the system which is not always easy to achieve. It calls for skills in coalition building, and in promoting cooperation between diverse interests. But probably the hardest part is making sure that the voices of those who are normally powerless and voiceless are heard. There is usually an abundance of experience at officer and councillor level in dealing with articulate and confident representatives of formal bodies in the private, public and voluntary sectors, but engaging with marginalised groups and with those excluded from mainstream society is altogether more demanding. It is in this sphere that community development has a particular contribution to make.

Experience has shown that it is vital that community development practitioners are given the maximum amount of independence in their work with local people. If they are seen as representatives of the 'system', they will quickly lose their credibility with some sections of the population. It is also important that they are not used simply to set up compliant groups of citizens, or to engage local people in partnerships, consultative bodies or other forums whose main purpose is to give them the appearance of legitimacy in terms of the involvement of local people. In the chapter on community development we issued a health warning about 'top down' approaches, and the danger of local groups being absorbed into partnerships where their influence is minimal.

The links between local government, governance and participatory democracy are problematic. The position is not helped by the fact that those who inform us on these matters tend to come from different traditions. Generally, those who write about local government and governance have academic public administration backgrounds or else hold senior posts in the public sector. The much smaller number who write about citizen participation in direct and electoral democracy are usually people with a background in community development. Contributors on both 'sides' come to their tasks with integrity, but – to use a physical metaphor – they are usually separated by a narrow strip of ground. It is the territory of perspectives and values, and comprehension and empathy. There needs to be a synergy arising from these contrasting backgrounds.

Stewart (1996), a highly respected writer on local government and democracy, in one of his most recent contributions, displays the humility and openness which are conducive to productive dialogue. In referring to the 'government of uncertainty' he stresses the need for 'public learning', and for an interpretation of democracy which extends beyond the ballot box. He acknowledges that local authorities have sought citizen involvement on their own terms, and have failed to work with 'the grain of how people behave' (p.215). Some of his own suggested innovations for reviving the practice of democracy will have to be measured by this yardstick.

In this spirit of openness, we briefly identify problems which arise at the interface between local people – particularly those who are most deeply alienated – and local governance.

- Large numbers of people have still to be convinced that consultative processes are taken seriously by those who make decisions and dispense resources. This, in turn, has a bearing on who participates and who elects to stay outside the process.
- Usually the mechanisms introduced to extend participation tend to attract the most articulate, the most confident, and those who are least pressured socially and economically. And, of course, the self-appointed spokesperson for the people! Hence, they are not completely representative.
- In examples of local governance there is rarely any reference to the differences between the participants in terms of the power that they represent. It is easy to see that local governance appears to be working effectively if a wide range of interests are represented around the table, but the subtleties of power and influence together with missing interests (for example, teenagers, homeless people, a minority ethnic group, homeworkers) can easily be overlooked or ignored.
- Even when groups experiencing social exclusion are brought into the forums of local governance, they do not operate on a level playing field. Such bodies consist mainly of professional workers, local politicians, representatives of business and voluntary organisations who will be employing skills they use every day. But representatives of other people will be operating in an entirely new cultural environment. For many it will be a daunting and – sometimes – intimidating experience. At issue here is not contrasting abilities but contrasting life experiences.
- When the emphasis is upon the middle ground in politics, and when class differences are being played down and consensual approaches elevated, the danger is that groups which do not conform to this new prescription will be excluded from the process of local governance. How, for example, does local governance accommodate marginalised groups who sometimes vent their frustration out on the streets? And what about Animal Rights Groups, Reclaim the Streets activists and groups of road protesters?

Problems like these lead some people involved in community development to advocate a 'twin track' approach. That is: while local authorities proceed with developing forms of governance which reflect their own changing role and which take account of the more pluralist distribution of power, local people – particularly those living in areas of multiple deprivation – should develop their own groups, forums and coalitions. These would remain independent and engage in negotiations with the local authority and other external bodies when necessary. They would control the agenda, and operate in a context in which they felt comfortable.

There are some similarities between this approach and that of Community Organising to which reference was made in the previous chapter. As a model, it has its attractions. It avoids the danger of incorporation into 'top-down' structures, and the risk of being marginalised in an alien setting. It also means that what happens at a community level is not so dependent upon the political control of the council, or upon its strategy.

However, it also brings its own problems. Community based structures of this type are not easy to create, and sustaining them can absorb people's time and energy to such an extent that their original objectives become sidelined. They are also not immune from the problems which can beset all organisations. The adoption of such a model could only be achieved with considerable financial help and also with intensive support from community development workers. The jury is still out on the most effective way for communities to organise, and in the end the responses are likely to reflect the diversity, the commitment and the attitudes of local people. That is probably how it should be.

Concluding Comments

Reducing the democratic deficit is likely to prove more difficult than reducing the balance of payments deficit, but we believe that the way to begin is by creating the conditions in which civil society can prosper. The imaginative ideas being put forward for reviving interest in representative democracy are more likely to meet with success if they are accompanied by measures to increase people's confidence in the value of participation in civic affairs generally.

The same is true of local governance. It requires a society in which the spirit of mutuality is sustained through a network of lively groups based upon identity, locality and special interests. Though the desire must be for co-operation, there must also be the capacity to deal with conflicts on the basis of equity, tolerance and respect. One of the functions of local government must be to intervene in order to uphold such values.

At first it might seem that communitarianism has an important contribution to make to the creation of a vibrant civil society, and this probably accounts for its appeal to a wide range of people concerned with building strong communities. It will be clear from earlier chapters that we do not share this view. The American version of communitarianism imported into this country has nothing of substance to offer those suffering forms of exclusion. They are exhorted to honour their obligations but not to campaign for their rights; to improve their 'communities' but not to make demands on the state. Though much of what passes for communitarian practice is unexceptionable, there are other features of it which are authoritarian and reactionary. Communitarianism is more of a cul-de-sac than a way forward.

Community development, on the other hand, is well established as a way of working with people collectively. Experience has taught it to be realistic in its expectations, and pragmatic in its approach. It is not prescriptive, but operates with the grain of people's experience. It recognises that rights and responsibilities belong together, and that both elements are equally important when it comes to promoting the spirit of mutuality and co-operation. We believe that it can help to create the conditions in which the democratic deficit can be reduced.

References

Archbishop's Commission on Rural Areas (1990) *Faith in the Countryside* (London: Churchman Publishing)

Archbishop's Commission on Urban Priority Areas (1985) *Faith in the City* (London: Church House Publishing)

Association of Metropolitan Councils (1989) *Community Development: The Local Authority Role* (Luton: LGMB publications)

Association of Metropolitan Councils (1993) *Local Authorities and Community Development: A Strategic Opportunity for the 1990s* (Luton: LGMB Publications)

Atkinson, D. (1994) *The Common Sense of Community* (London: Demos)

Barr, A. (1996b) *Practising Community Development: Experience in Strathclyde* (Revised Edition) (London: CDF/SCDC)

Barr, A., Drysdale, J. and Henderson, P. (1997) *Towards Caring Communities? Community Development and Community Care* (Brighton: Pavilion)

Barr, A., Hamilton, R. and Purcell, R. (1996c) *Learning for Change: Community Education and Community Development* (London: CDF/SCDC)

Barr, A., Hashagen, S. and Purcell, R. (1996) *Measuring Community Development in Northern Ireland* (Belfast: Department of Health and Social Services)

Benington, J. (1974) 'Strategies for change at the local level: some reflections' in *Community Work One*, Jones, D. and Mayo, M. (eds) (London: Routledge)

—— (1996) 'New Paradigms and Practices for Local Government: Capacity Building in Civil Society' in *The Politics of Attachment* Skinner, S. and Roberts, J. (eds) (London: Free Association Books)

Burns, D. et al (1994) *The Politics of Decentralisation: Revitalising Local Democracy* (Basingstoke: Macmillan)

Butcher, H. and Mullard, M. (1993) 'Community Policy, Citizenship and Democracy' in *Community and Public Policy* Butcher, H. et al. (eds) (London: Pluto/CDF/BICC)

Campbell, B. (1993) *Goliath* (London: Methuen)

—— (1995) 'Old Fogeys and Angry Young Men: A Critique of Communitarianism', *Soundings*, Issue I

Campfens, H. (ed.) (1997) *Community Development Around the World* (Toronto: University of Toronto)

CDF (1997) *Guidelines to the Community Involvement Aspect of the SRB Challenge Fund* (London: CDF)

Chanan, G. (1994) *Discovering Community Action* (London: CDF)

Cohen (1997) 'Beyond the Community Romance', *Soundings*, Issue 5

Coleman, J. (1957) *Community Conflict* (New York: The Free Press)

Commission for Local Democracy (1995) *Taking Charge: The Rebirth of Democracy* (London: *Municipal Journal*)

Commission on Social Justice (1994) *Social Justice Strategies for National Renewal* (London: Vintage)

Creighton, S. (ed.) (1996) *Environment Action Pack: Practical Ideas for Community Organisations* (London: Community Matters/CDF)

Curtin, C. (1996) 'Back to the Future? Communities and Rural Poverty' in *Poverty in Rural Ireland*, Curtin, C. et al. (eds) (Dublin: Oak Tree Press)

Demaine, J. (1996) *Beyond Communitarianism: Citizenship, Politics and Education* (Basingstoke: Macmillan)

Dennis, N. (1996) *The Invention of Permanent Poverty* (London: Institute of Economic Affairs)

Dennis, N. and Erdos, G. (1992) *Families Without Fatherhood* (London: Institute of Economic Affairs)

Dennis, N. and Halsey, A. H. (1988) *English Ethical Socialism* (Oxford: Oxford University Press)

Derber, C. (1995) quoted by Steel, J. in 'Clinton policies are caught in communitarian crossfire', *The Guardian* (12 April 1995)

Etzioni, A. (1993) *The Spirit of Community* (Crown Prince Publishers) (English edition 1995, Fontana Press)

—— (1995a) *The Parenting Deficit* (London: Demos)

—— (1995b) 'Common Values' in *New Statesman & Society* (12 May 1995)

—— (1997) *The New Golden Rule: Community and Morality in a Democratic Society* (London: Profile Books Ltd)

Farrar, M. (1996) 'Black communities and processes of exclusion' in *Corporate City? Partnership, Participation and Partition in Urban Development in Leeds* Haughton, G. and Williams, C.C. (eds) (Aldershot: Avebury)

Frazer, E. (1996) 'The Value of Locality' in *Rethinking Local Democracy* King, D. and Stoker, G. (eds) (Basingstoke: Macmillan)

Frazer, E. and Lacey, N. (1993) *The Politics of Community: A Feminist Critique of the Liberal-Communitarian Debate* (London: Harvester Wheatsheaf)

Galbraith, J. K. (1996) *The Good Society: The Human Agenda* (London: Sinclaire-Stevenson)

Geddes, M. (1995) *Poverty, Excluded Communities and Local Democracy* CLD research report No. 9 (Commission for Local Democracy)

—— (1996) *Extending Democratic Practice in Local Government*, CLD research report No. 17 (Commission for Local Democracy)

Gibson, T. (1996) *The Power in Our Hands* (Oxon: Jon Carpenter)

Gray, J. (1995) *Berlin* (London: Fontana)

—— (1996) *After Social Democracy: Politics, Capitalism and the Common Life* (London: Demos)

Harris, R. (1992) *The Conservative Community* (London: Centre for Policy Studies)

Hart, R. (1997) *Children's Participation* (London: Earthscan)

Henderson, P. and Salmon, H (1995) *Community Organising – The UK Context* (London: CDF/Churches Community Work Alliance)

Henderson, P. (ed.) (1995) *Children and Communities* (London: Pluto Press/CDF/The Childrens' Society)

Henderson, P. (1997) *Social Inclusion and Citizenship in Europe – The Contribution of Community Development* (The Hague: Combined European Bureau for Social Development)

Holman, B. (1997) *FARE Dealing: Neighbourhood Involvement in a Housing Scheme* (London: CDF)

Hughes ,G. (1996) 'Communitarianism and law and order', *Critical Social Policy* 49 (London: Sage Publications)

Leach, S. Davies, H. and Associates (1996) *Enabling or Disabling Local Government* (Buckingham: Open University Press)

Leadbeater, C. (1996) *The Self-Policing Society* (London: Demos)

Marshall, T. H. (1950) *Citizenship and Social Class and Other Essays* (Cambridge: Cambridge University Press)

May (1997) *Challenging Assumptions: Gender Considerations in Urban Regeneration in the UK* (Oxon: Oxfam)

Mayo, M. and Craig, G. (eds) (1995) *Community Empowerment* (London: Zed Books)

Meekosha, H. (1993) 'The Bodies Politic – Equality, Difference and Community practice' in *Community and Public Policy*, Butcher, H. et al. (eds) (London: Pluto Press/CDF/BICC)

Mulgan, G. (1995) 'Beyond the Lure of Off-the-Shelf Ethics', *The Independent* 30 January 1995

Murray, L. (1996) 'Personal and Social Influences on Parenting and Adult Adjustment' in *The Politics of Attachment* Kramer, S. and Roberts, J. (eds) (London: Free Association Books)

Pahl, R. (1996) 'Friendly Society' in *The Politics of Attachment*, Kramer, S. and Roberts, J. (eds) (London: Free Association Books)

Phillips, M. (1995) 'Comment', *The Observer* (2 April 1995)

Prior, J. et al (1995) *Citizenship: Rights, Community and Participation* (London: Pitman)

Putnam, R.D. (1993) *Making Democracy Work: Civic Traditions in Modern Italy* (Princeton: Princeton University Press)

Roome, N. (1993) 'Green Perspectives on Community and Public Policy' in *Community and Public Policy*, Butcher, H. et al. (eds) (London: Pluto Press/ CDF/BICC)

Russell, H. (1995) *Poverty Close to Home* (London: Mowbray)

Shucksmith, M. et al (1994) *Disadvantage in Rural Scotland* (Aberdeen: University of Aberdeen)

Simey, M. (1995) 'The Politics of Social Change' in *Local Work* No. 66 (October) (Manchester: CLES)

Skinner, S. (1997) *Building Community Strengths: A Resource Book on Capacity Building* (London: CDF)

Steele, J. (1995) 'Clinton policies are caught in Communitarian crossfire', *The Guardian* (12 April 1995)

Stewart, J. (1996) 'Thinking Collectively in the Public Domain', *Soundings*, Issue 4.

Stewart, M. and Taylor, M. (1995) *Empowerment and Estate Regeneration* (Bristol: The Policy Press)

Tam, H. (1995) 'Communitarianism: What is it all about?' *SCCD News*, Issue 13

Tam, H. (ed.) (1995) *The Citizens Agenda* (Cambridge: White Horse Press)

—— (1996) *Punishment, Excuses and Moral Development* (Aldershot: Avebury)

Taylor, C. (1995) *Philosophical Arguments* (Massachusetts: Harvard University Press)

Taylor, M. (1995) 'Community Work and the State: The Changing Context of UK Practice' in *Community Empowerment* Craig, G. and Mayo, M. (eds) (London: Zed Books)

—— (1997) 'Community-based responses to urban deprevation and social exclusion in the UK' in Henderson, P. (ed.), *Setting the Scene: Community-Based Respones to Urban Deprevation in Five European countries* (Leeds: Combined European Bureau for Social Development)

Thomas, D.N. (1996) *Oil on Troubled Waters* (London: Directory of Social Change)

Thornton, P. (1996) *Management Development for Community Practice* (Leeds: CDF)

Tyrell (1995) 'Me Versus Us' in *Cities of Pride*, Atkinson, D. (ed.) (London: Cassell)

Ungerson, C. (1992) 'Caring and Citizenship: a Complex Relationship' in *Community Care – a Reader* (Basingstoke: Macmillan)

Wahlberg, M. et al. (1995) *Enhancing Local Democracy* (Luton: Local Government Management Board)

Wilkinson, H. and Mulgan, G. (1995) *Freedom's Children: Work, Relationships and Politics for 18–34-Year-Olds in Britain Today* (London: Demos)

Willetts, D. (1993) *Civic Conservatism* (London: Social Market Foundation)

Wilson, M. (1995) 'Communitarianism: A critique', *SCCD News*, Issue 13